Open-Ended Art

Written by **Kathy Douglas**
Illustrated by **Barb Tourtillotte**

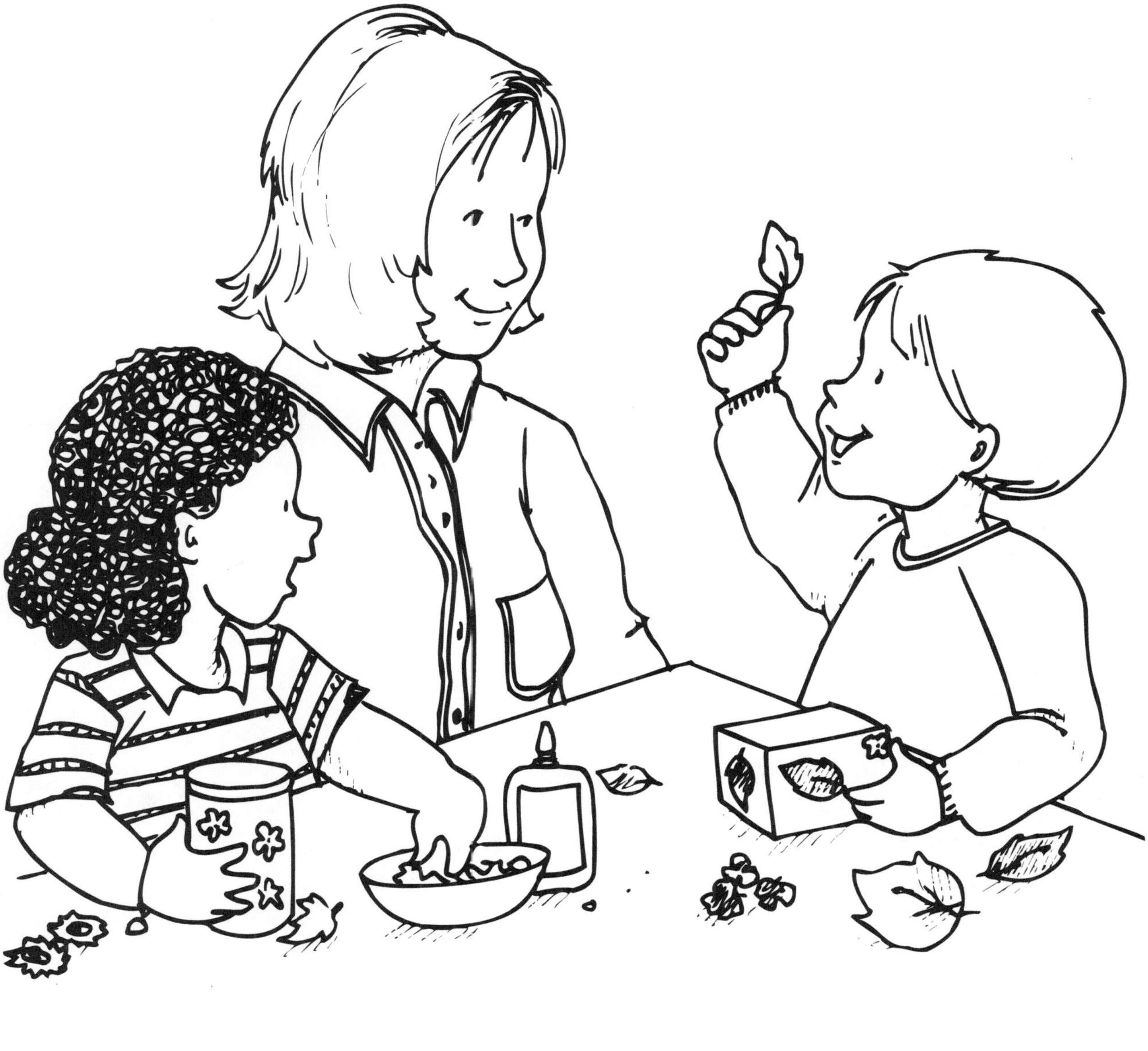

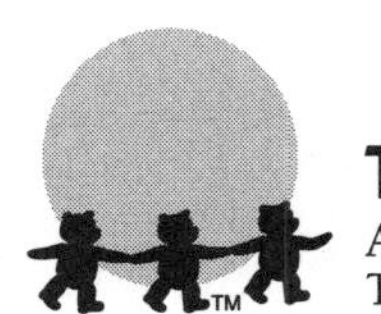

Totline® Publications
A Division of Frank Schaffer Publications, Inc.
Torrance, California

Managing Editor: Mina McMullin
Contributing Editor: Jean Warren
Copyeditor: Kathy Zaun
Editorial Assistant: Mary Newmaster
Graphic Designer (Interior): Jill Kaufman
Graphic Designer (Cover): Brenda Mann Harrison
Illustrator (Cover): Barb Tourtillotte
Production Manager: Janie Schmidt

ISBN: 1-57029-284-1

Printed in the United States of America
Published by Totline® Publications
23740 Hawthorne Blvd.
Torrance, CA 90505

Introduction

Art can be a wonderful experience for children when they are given the opportunity to create by experimenting with a number of different art tools. This type of art focuses on the processes involved in creating rather than the finished project.

Open-Ended Art is filled with an exciting variety of ideas and art projects that have been designed to allow children the freedom to create by means of open-ended activities and a wide variety of tools. Some of the tools involved include these:

drawing tools: colored pencils, crayons in a variety of colors, non-toxic markers, chalk

painting materials: paintbrushes, leaves or other nature items, combs

sculpting tools: twigs, craft sticks

gluing materials: glue, glitter glue, glue-water mixture

weaving and sewing materials: ribbon, yarn, string

miscellaneous materials: buttons, rickrack, paint pens, glue sticks, food coloring

To effectively allow children to freely experiment and create and to maximize their experiences with the activities in this book, set up a process-oriented environment. This can be easily done. Simply provide a large variety of each kind of tool needed for a project. For example, if an activity calls for paint, paintbrushes, and paper, set out many different colors of paint, many different sizes and widths of brushes, and a variety of different papers (vary size, texture, color, etc.). These options allow for interesting differences the children can later observe and help the children look at things in a different way.

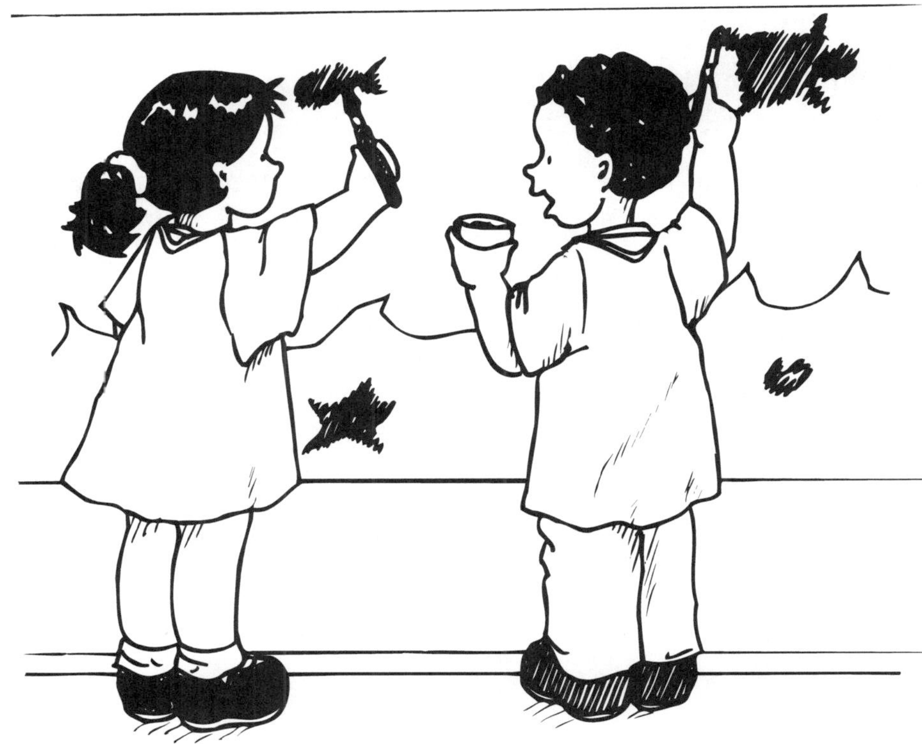

As you work with the children on the activities in *Open-Ended Art*, you are sure to come up with other art ideas you might like to try. Implement these ideas and watch as the children's creativity and imaginations begin to grow. However, before you begin, read through the tips on the following two pages.

Introduction continued

Tips for Working With Preschoolers

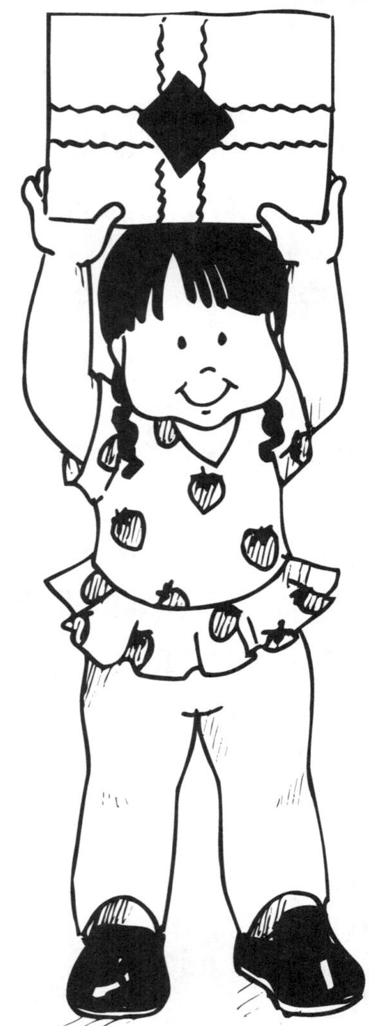

- Encourage the children with positive feedback that is not judgmental. (Examples: "I see you chose a lot of yellow paint for your painting." "Tell me how you formed this piece of clay.")
- Young children are process-oriented by nature. The end product is usually not what is important to the child.
- All art activities should be age-appropriate. Be sure to keep in mind each child's motor skills and cognitive abilities.
- Art development is universal. All children go through the four stages of development in the preschool years: basic scribbles, controlled scribbles, suns, and human figures.
- Children's art should be their own work, not the teacher's predetermined outcome.
- Models that teachers draw and coloring sheets take away from a child's freedom to create.
- Ask the children where they would like their names printed on their art creations.
- During circle time, discuss the artwork that the children have done each day.
- Provide a wide range of materials for children to choose from.
- Cut paper into different shapes and sizes to give the children a different perspective.
- Children are naturally imaginative and creative. Teachers can foster this through open-ended art experiences.
- Giving children choices helps teach them problem solving and thinking skills.

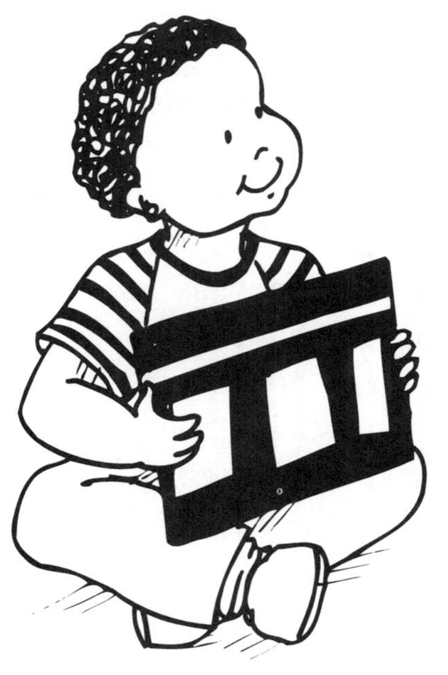

Introduction continued

Displaying Open-Ended Art

Both children and adults enjoy looking at art. An early childhood classroom becomes more interesting and expressive when the children's art is displayed in a creative manner. Follow the tips below to create eye-catching displays.

- Hang the children's art at the children's eye level.
- Children's art should be displayed in an attractive manner.
- Large cardboard boxes are good display centers and can be placed outside the classroom door so parents can view with their children the projects that are created.
- Have the children create frames to display art.
- Hang artwork on mirrors.
- Write the stories or titles of work on index cards and hang them behind the pictures or creations.
- Hang artwork outside the classroom on hallway walls.
- If you have a gazebo, hang the art outside in the gazebo for an art show.
- Use a clothesline and clothespins hung at the children's eye level for a display option.
- During the holidays, display art on a backdrop representing the season.
- String holiday lights on boards to display art.
- Gift-wrap is a good background for seasonal art and for everyday art.
- Scan children's art and e-mail it to their parents.
- Create a children's art garden by sticking yardsticks in the ground and hanging their art on the yardsticks. Parents will surely enjoy this display.
- The children can draw small pictures on index cards and make crowns out of their art. The children can wear the crowns home.

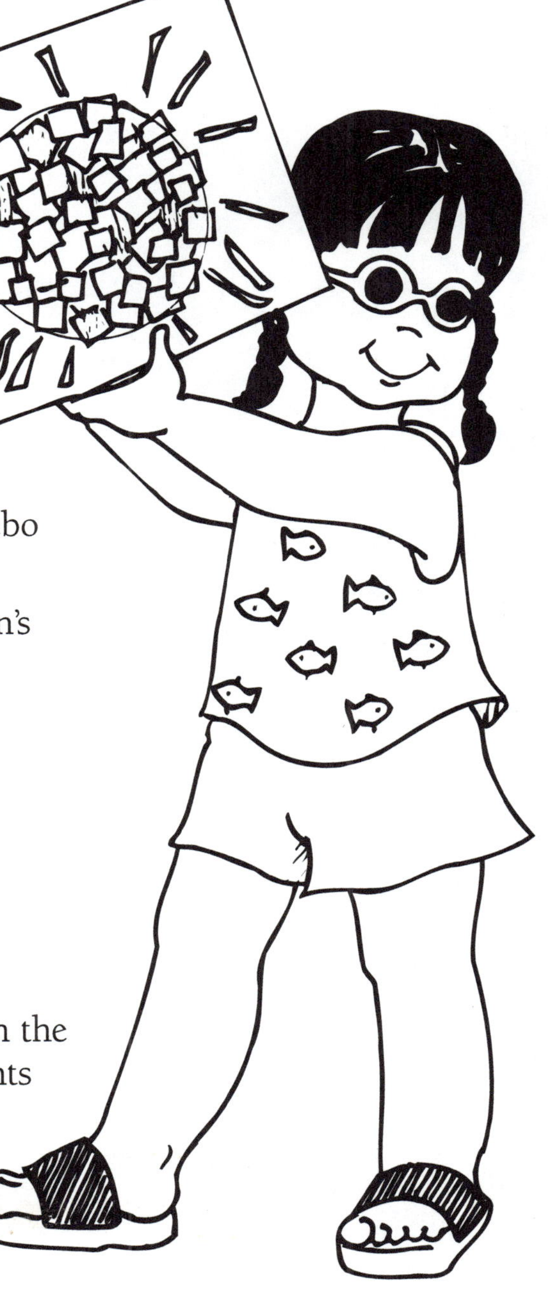

Contents

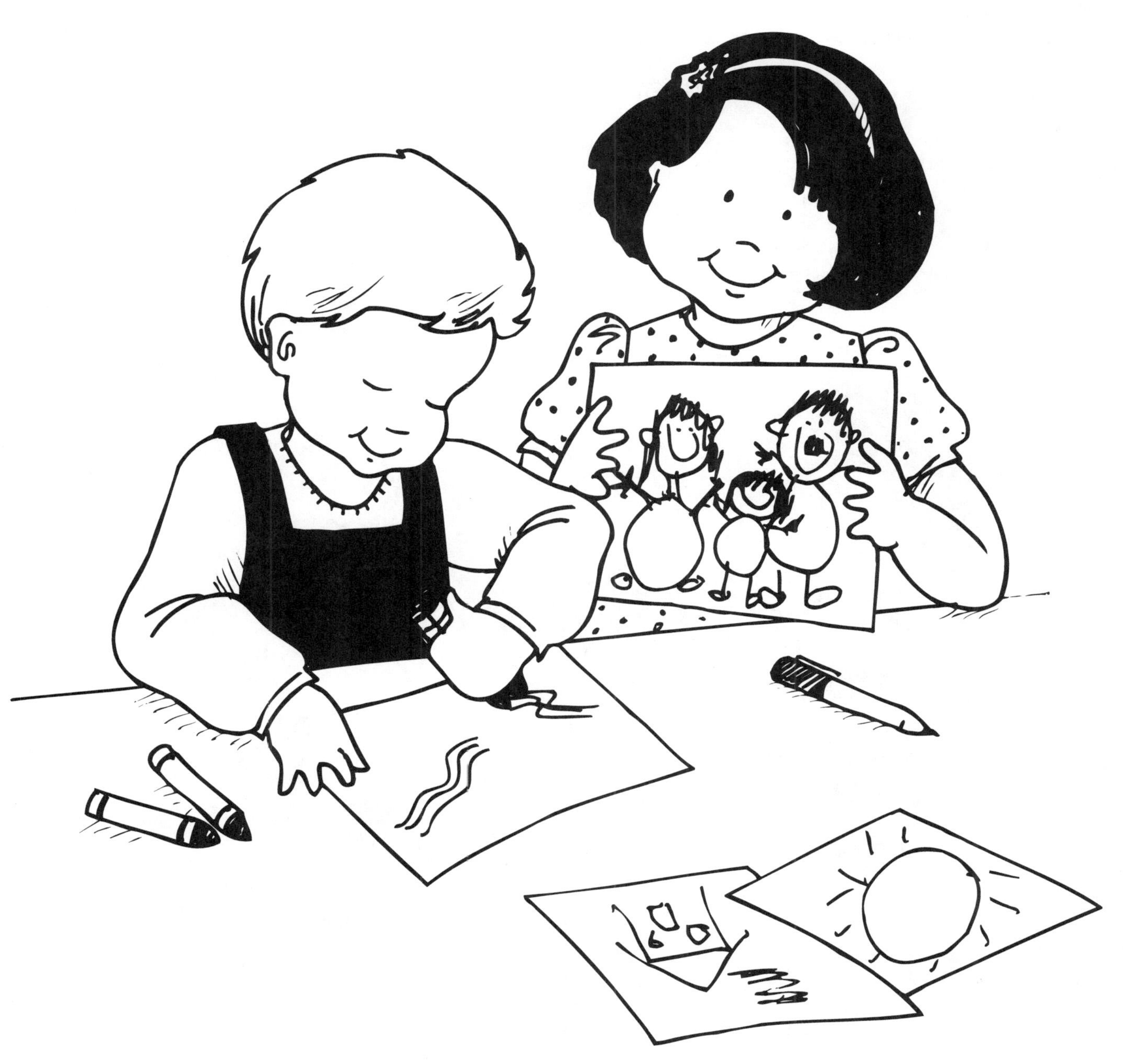

Drawing

Silly Eggs

This is a fun spring activity, farm activity, Easter project, or art project.

Place one or two hard-boiled eggs in a carton for each child doing the activity. Have the children use markers or crayons to draw colorful patterns, designs, or pictures on their eggs. Label the children's eggs with labels or sticky notes.

Quick Tip

Hardboil the eggs the day before you do this activity with the children. Be sure to make extra eggs in case some break or are dropped.

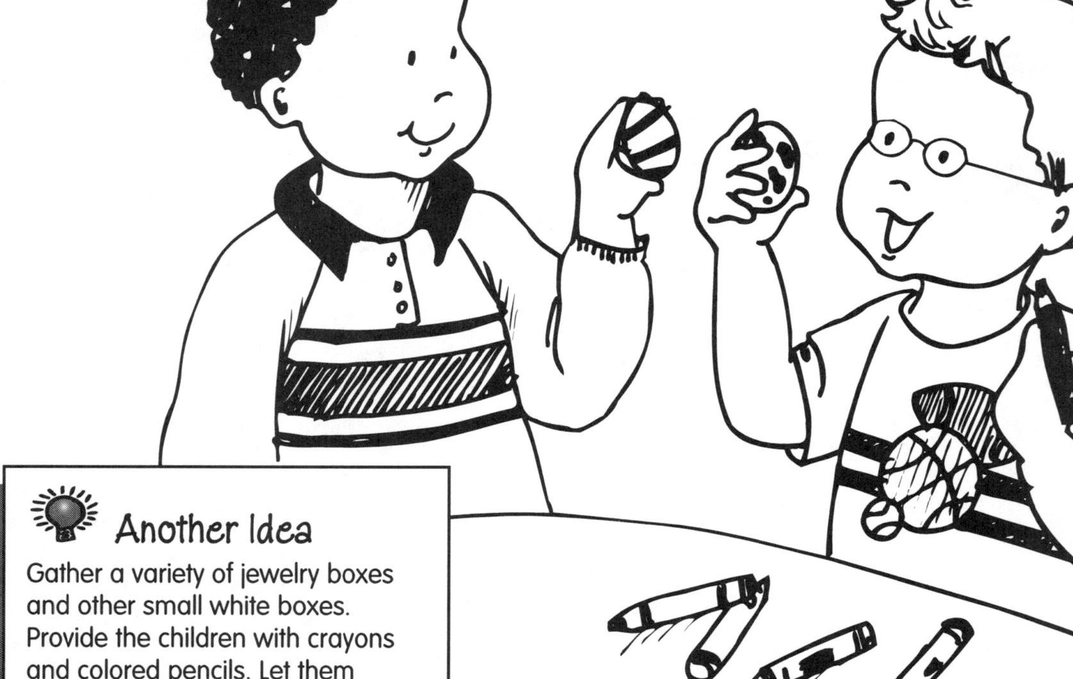

Another Idea

Gather a variety of jewelry boxes and other small white boxes. Provide the children with crayons and colored pencils. Let them create gift boxes or decorative boxes for themselves, their families, or their friends. During circle time, discuss what they would choose to put inside their boxes.

Tower Power

This activity requires a variety of boxes that range in size so that they can be easily stacked on top of each other to form a tower. You will want to prepare enough boxes so that groups of four children can work together to build towers. Cover each box with wrapping paper, or tape different types of paper to the sides of the boxes.

Have the children stack the boxes from largest to smallest. (Be sure that the towers are no higher than the children's eye level and that the top box is low enough for the children to draw on.) After they are stacked, tape the boxes together by applying masking tape either inside the boxes or neatly on the outside of the boxes.

Encourage the children to draw pictures of nature, friends, or just bright designs. Display the towers in the classroom and school with the children's names printed on another piece of paper and attached to the towers.

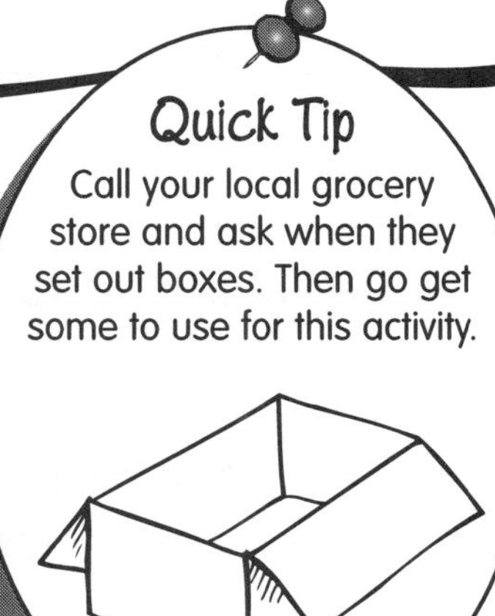

Quick Tip

Call your local grocery store and ask when they set out boxes. Then go get some to use for this activity.

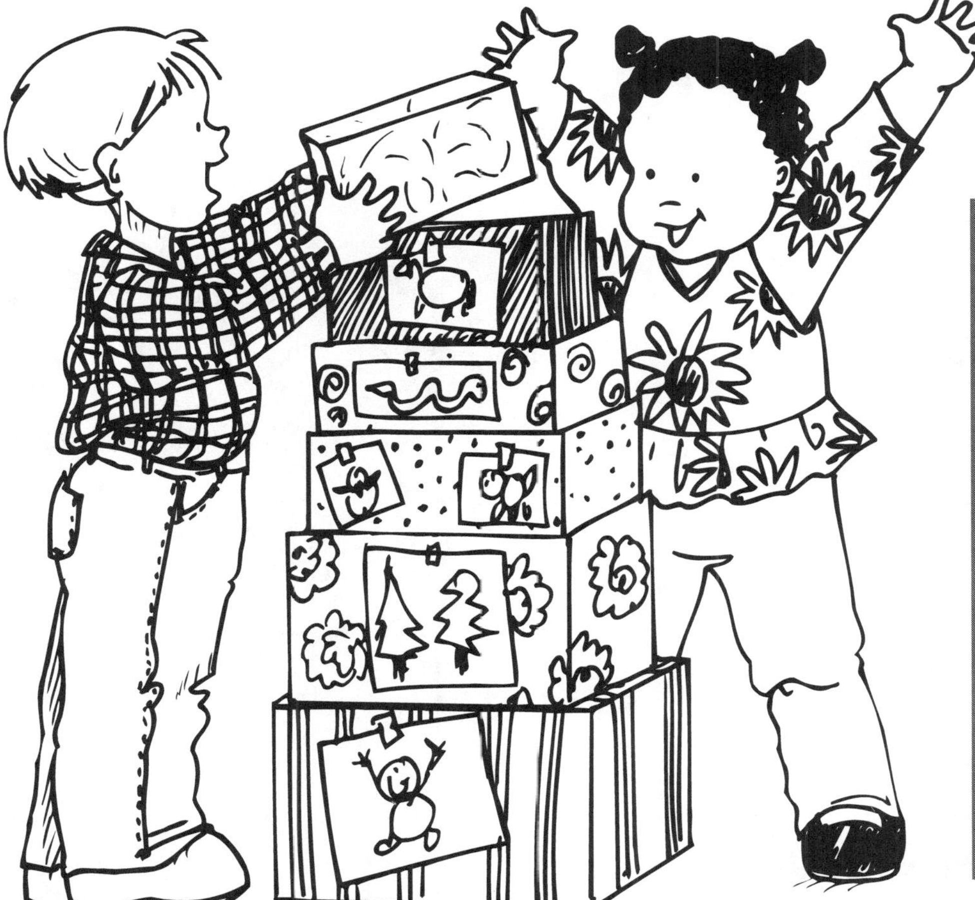

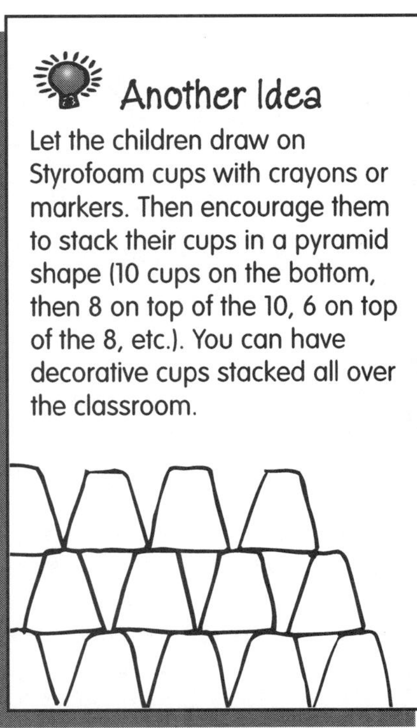

Another Idea

Let the children draw on Styrofoam cups with crayons or markers. Then encourage them to stack their cups in a pyramid shape (10 cups on the bottom, then 8 on top of the 10, 6 on top of the 8, etc.). You can have decorative cups stacked all over the classroom.

Add-Ons

Let the children look through magazines and find pictures to cut out and glue onto paper. As they do this, encourage them to add to their pictures by drawing more flowers, people, water, or whatever they like around their cutouts. Ask the children where they want their names written on their pictures. Then have them tell you a story about their pictures as you write it down on their papers.

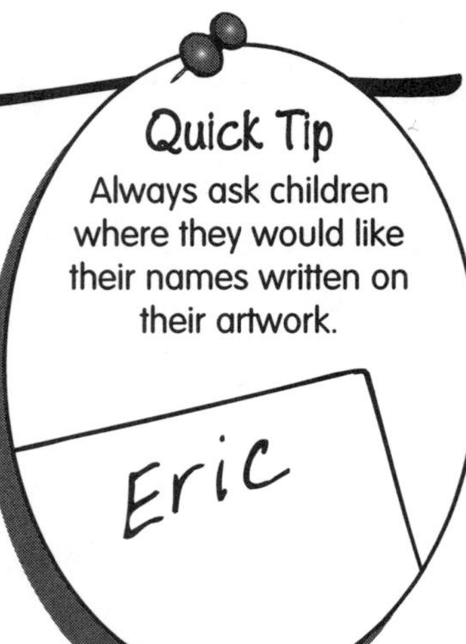

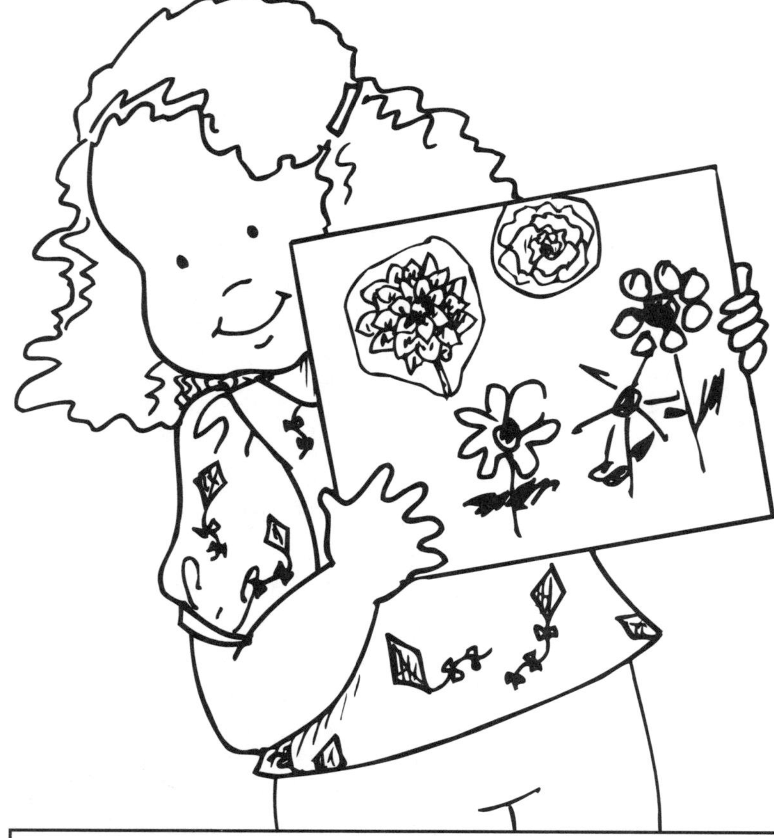

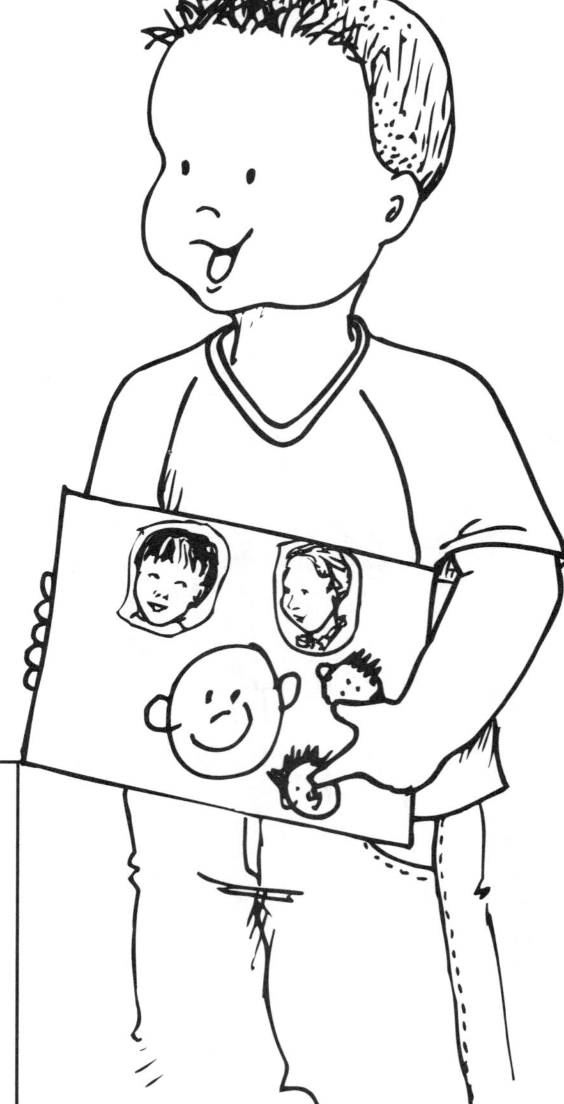

Another Idea

Have the children cut out only the heads of animals or people. They can then create the bodies using markers or crayons. Or, have the children cut out only the bodies and let them create the heads. They could also cut out tires of cars and create the cars. There is a wide range of possibilities the children could try.

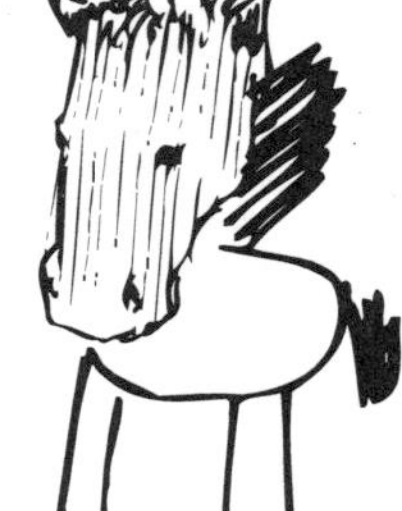

Twiggy Fun

Go for a walk with the children and look at all the different types of twigs on trees. On your walk, find twigs that have fallen and gather them with the children. (Be sure to include a variety of lengths and thicknesses.) On the playground or in the classroom, sort and classify the twigs. Set out paper on a table or sidewalk and put different colors of paint in easy-to-use containers. Show the children how to dip their twigs into the paint and draw pictures on their papers. Encourage the children to use a variety of lengths and thicknesses of twigs.

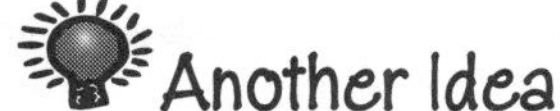

Another Idea

Get old-fashioned ink pens and ink wells from local secondhand shops. Let the children try an old method of drawing with ink. You may even be able to have someone from a local antique store come to the school to show the children old writing tools.

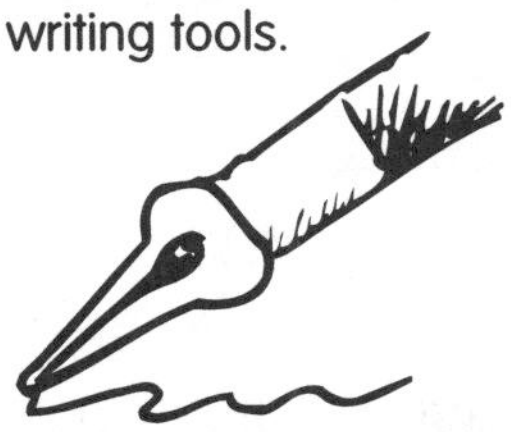

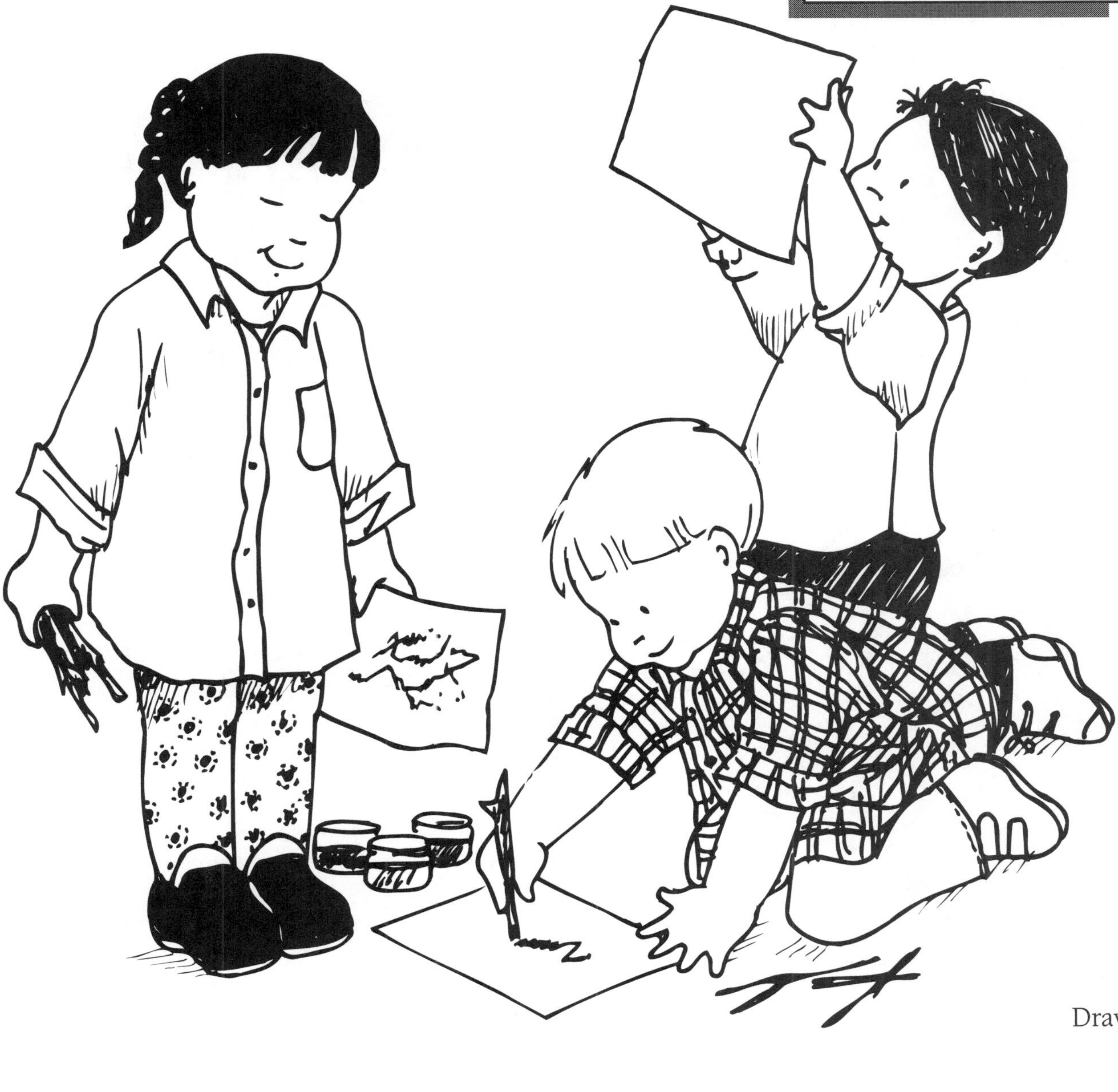

Fluffy Creations

Put some shaving cream into some mixing bowls. Make a few different colors of shaving cream by adding one drop of food coloring to each bowl and stirring. (Be sure to leave several bowls of cream white.) Set the cream out on your choice of surface—paper, Styrofoam trays, or a tabletop.

Put smocks on the children to keep their clothes dry and clean. The children will enjoy drawing in white or colored shaving cream with their fingers or with craft sticks to create different effects. Encourage them to spread shaving cream all over the table, trays, or paper. Let them mix colors and draw flowers, suns, birds, or whatever they desire. The children can also practice printing their names in the shaving cream by signing their artwork. When the children have finished their art creations, direct them to the sink and then show them where to hang their smocks.

Quick Tip

One drop of food coloring is all that is necessary for mixing with small amounts of shaving cream.

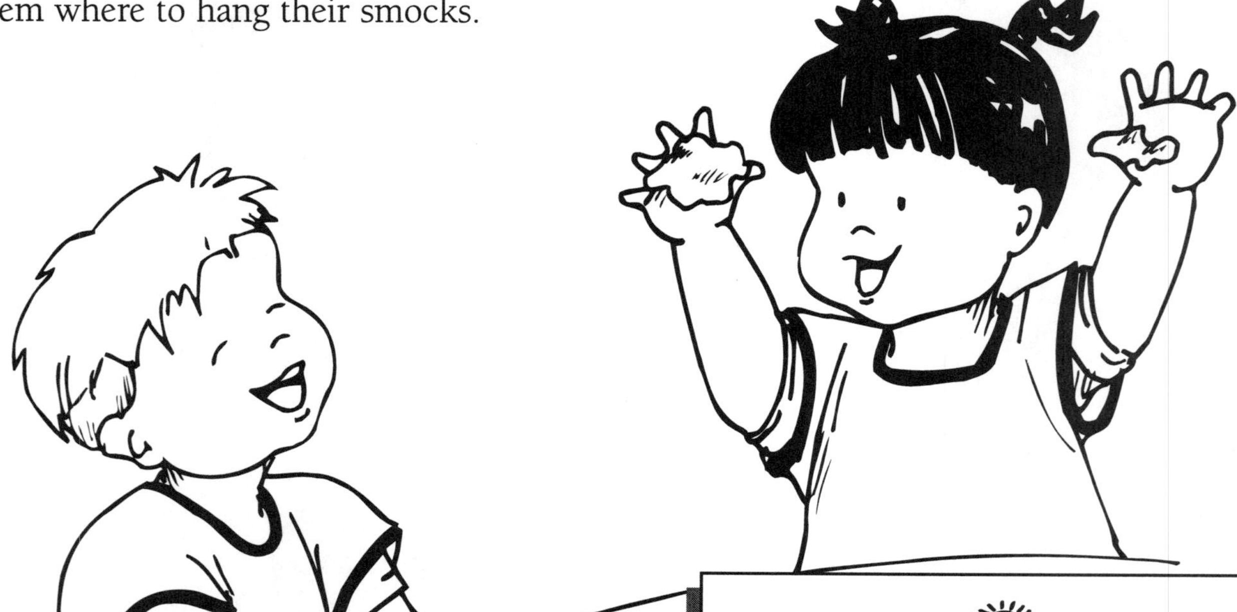

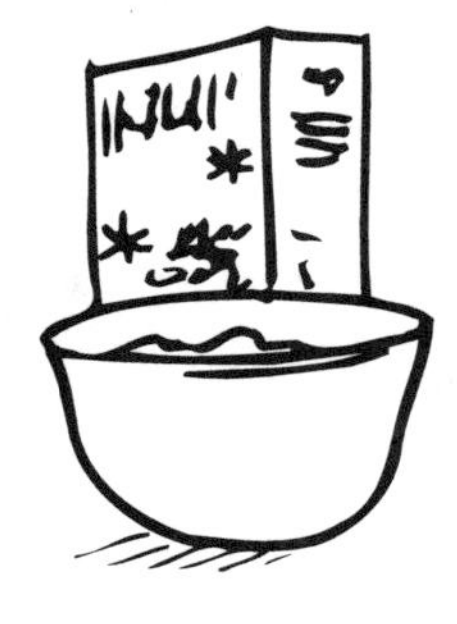

Another Idea

Use a different medium for the children to draw with, such as Ivory Snow and food coloring. Mix it up with small amounts of water and food coloring and let them use it in the same manner as the shaving cream. The texture and smell will provide the children with a different experience than the shaving cream.

Triple Doodle Fun

Gather markers and put them together in sets of three, using three different colors in each set. Place a rubber band around each set, with all ends facing the same way. Provide the children with many different shapes and sizes of paper. Show the children how to take the marker tops off and draw using the different-colored marker bundles.

Ask the children to show you what happens when they draw very slowly. Next, ask them what happens when they draw quickly, or when they draw in circles. Let the children select their own colors of markers after they experiment with the prepared bundles. You will need to help them put the rubber bands on their chosen markers. (You can also do Triple Doodle Fun using bundles of crayons or colored pencils.)

Hang up the splashy creations all over the room.

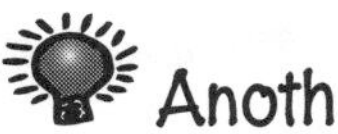

Another Idea

When the weather is warm and you want to do a Triple Doodle Foot Activity, have the children take off their shoes and socks. Set out enough large sheets of paper so that you can have four to six children at each sheet of paper. Next, let each child select three crayons, stick them between his or her toes, and then try doing Triple Doodle Art!

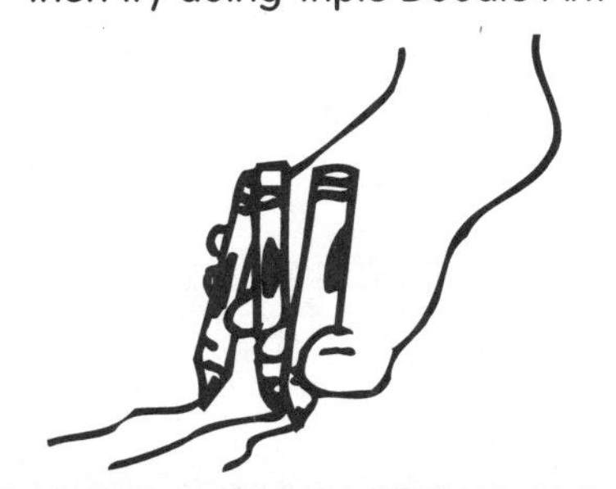

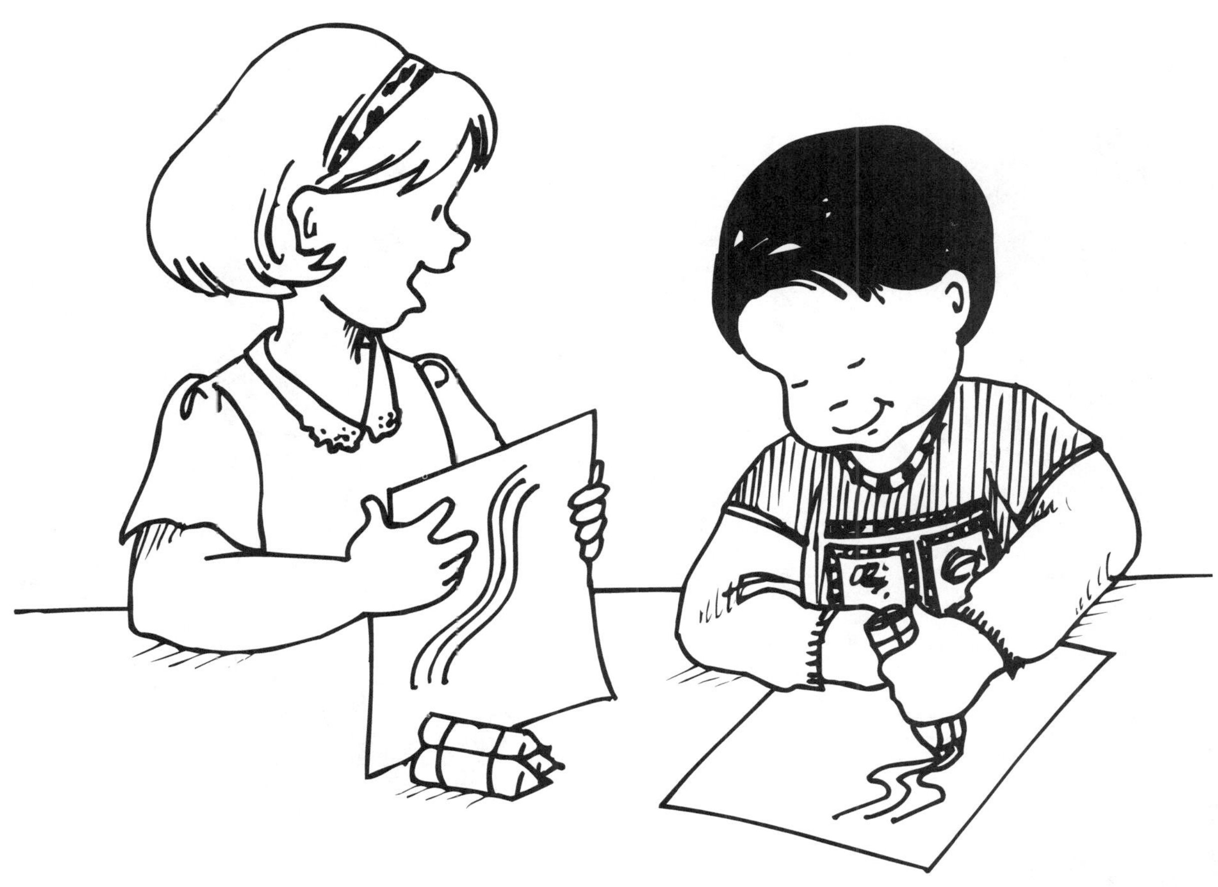

Flowing Art Creations

On a warm day, hang long sheets of white butcher paper all over the walls of a small area on the playground at the children's eye level. Set up a cassette player and have a variety of music (country, jazz, classical, rock, etc.) available. Tell the children that music makes us feel, think, and move. Have the children listen to some of the different kinds of music. (Children need to be 3 feet apart for freedom of movement for this activity.)

Provide the children with a basket of markers. Turn on the music and let the children draw on the paper while listening to the different types of music. Observe to see if there are different movements and drawing motions with the musical selections.

Let the children change colored markers as they like. Encourage the children to print their names on the flowing art creations.

Another Idea

Paper plates come in many shapes, sizes, and textures. They provide a wonderful way to introduce the idea of looking at things in a different way. Give the children paper plates they can draw pictures on using crayons, markers, and pencils. Encourage the children to create frames around their pictures by drawing on the edges of their plates.

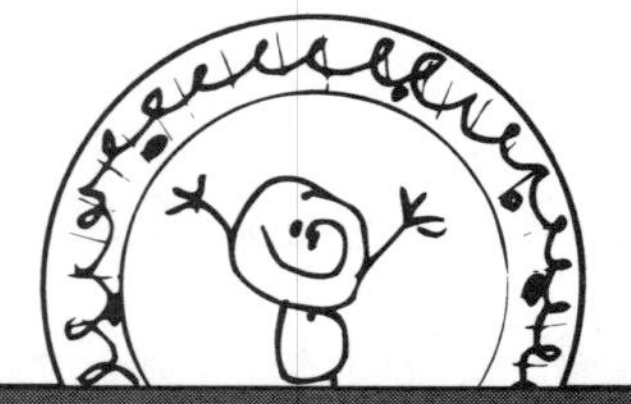

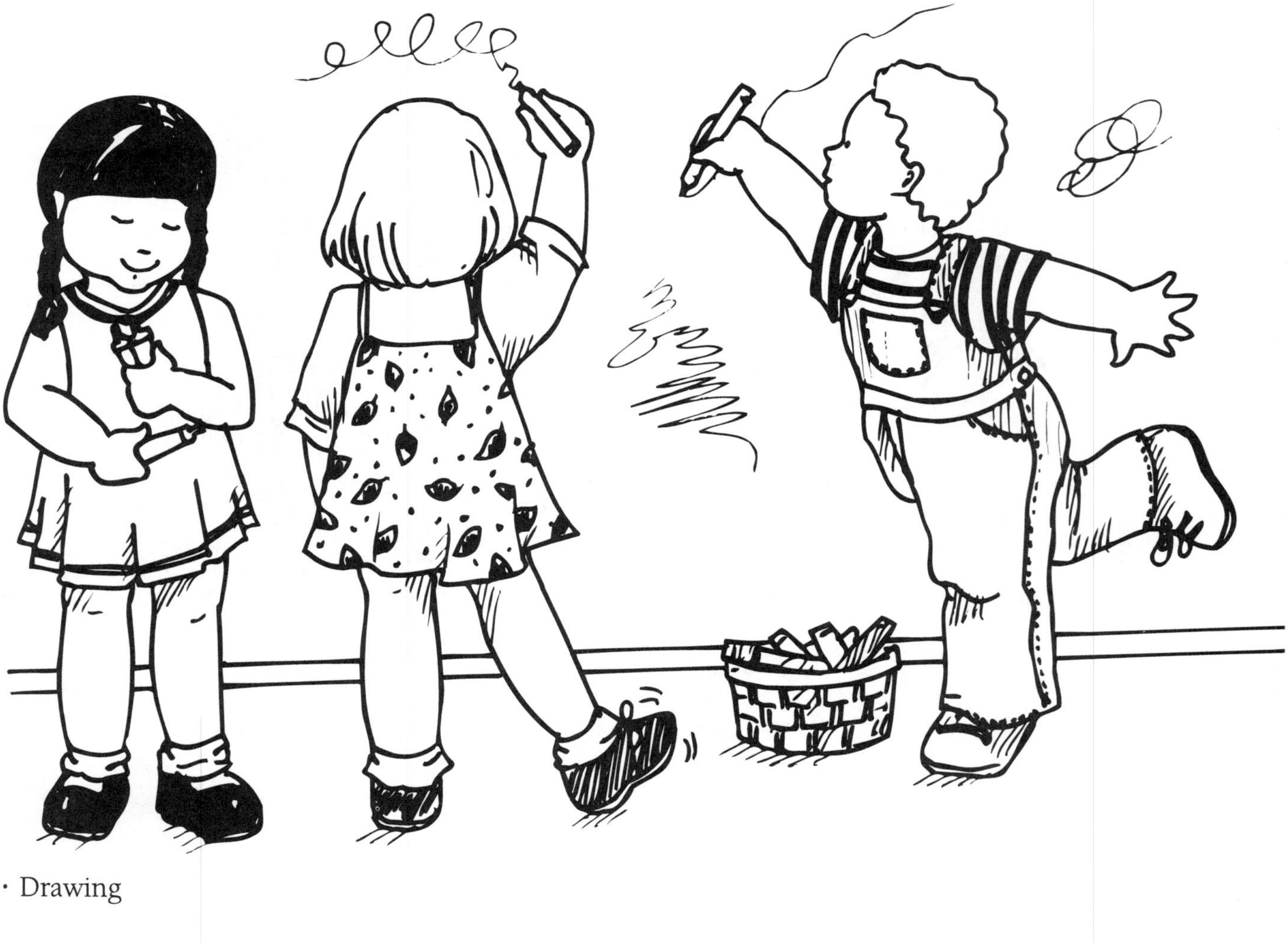

Colorful Sand Creations

This activity works well with groups of six children in the art center. Set out two plastic cups, each half full of white sand, on a Styrofoam tray for each child. Set several markers on each tray.

To demonstrate for the children, show them a cup of the white sand. Let them see that by taking a marker tip and stirring it round and round in the cup of sand, they can change the color of the sand. (You can tell the children that the fluid from the marker is being transferred to the sand, thus making it the color of the marker.)

When the children arrive at the art center, have them create colored sand in their cups and then dump it onto their trays. Tell the children to draw with their fingers in the different-colored sand they have created. Some children will merge the colors, while others will try to keep them separate.

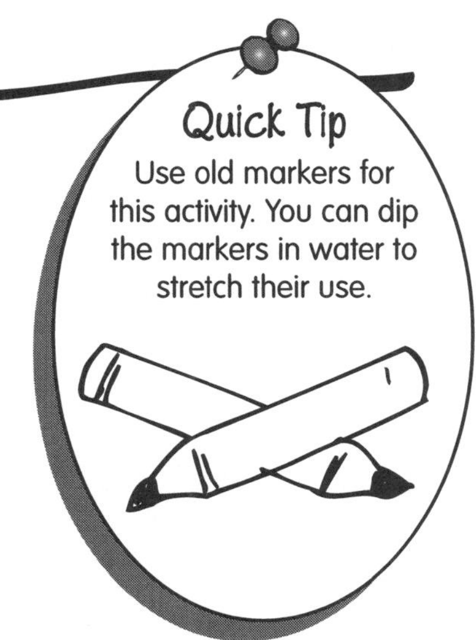

Quick Tip

Use old markers for this activity. You can dip the markers in water to stretch their use.

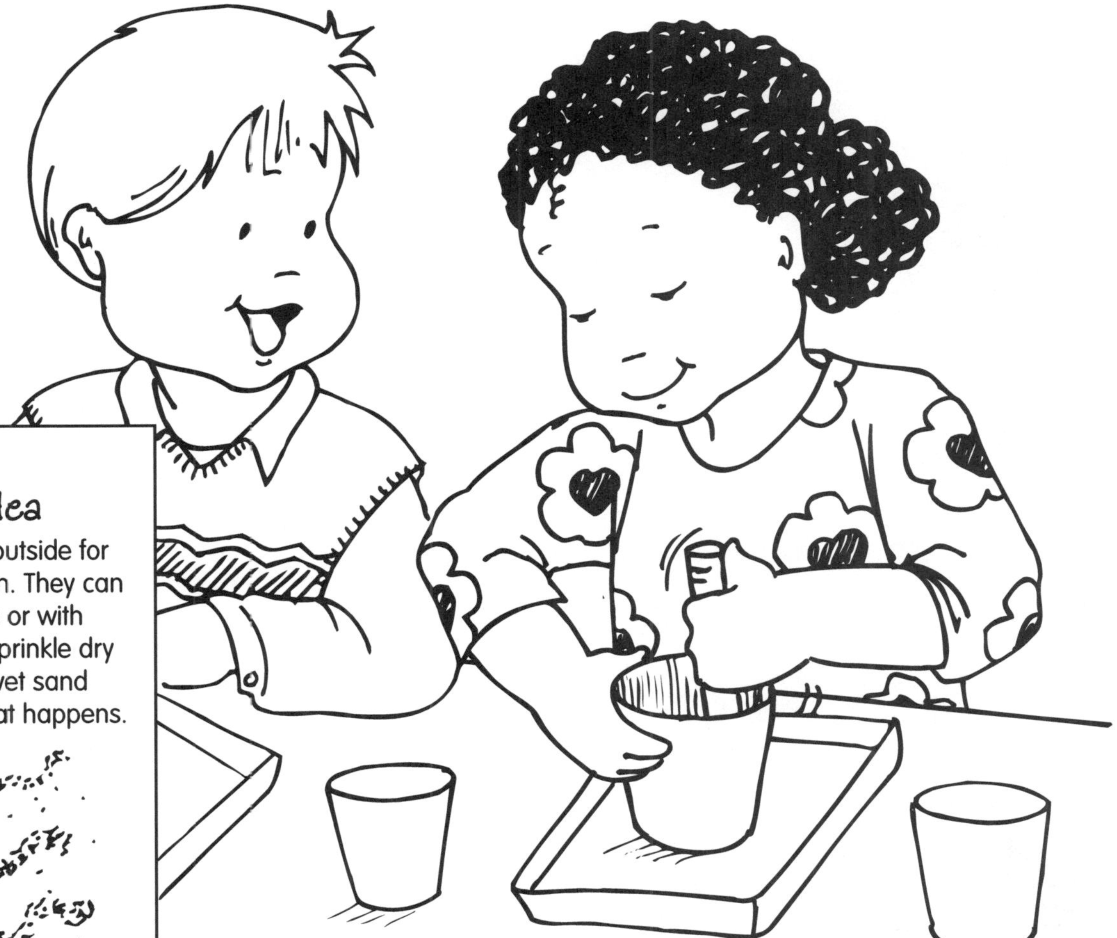

Another Idea

Set trays of wet sand outside for the children to draw on. They can draw with their fingers or with twigs. Next, let them sprinkle dry white sand into their wet sand drawings and see what happens.

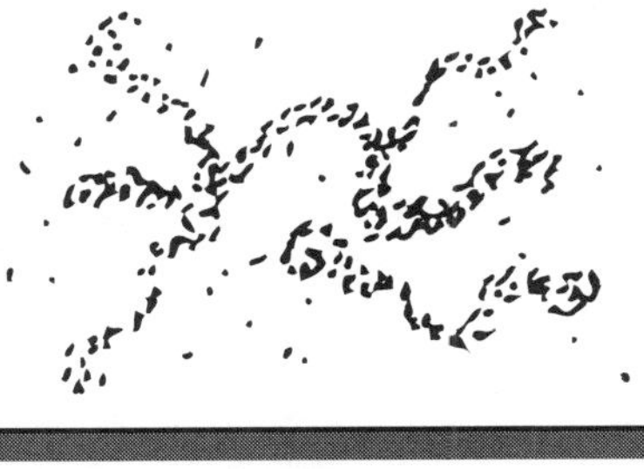

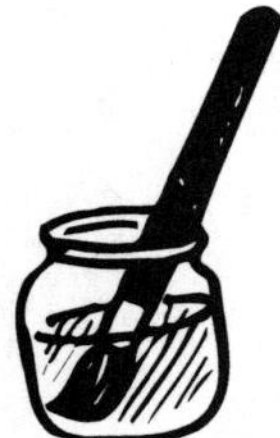

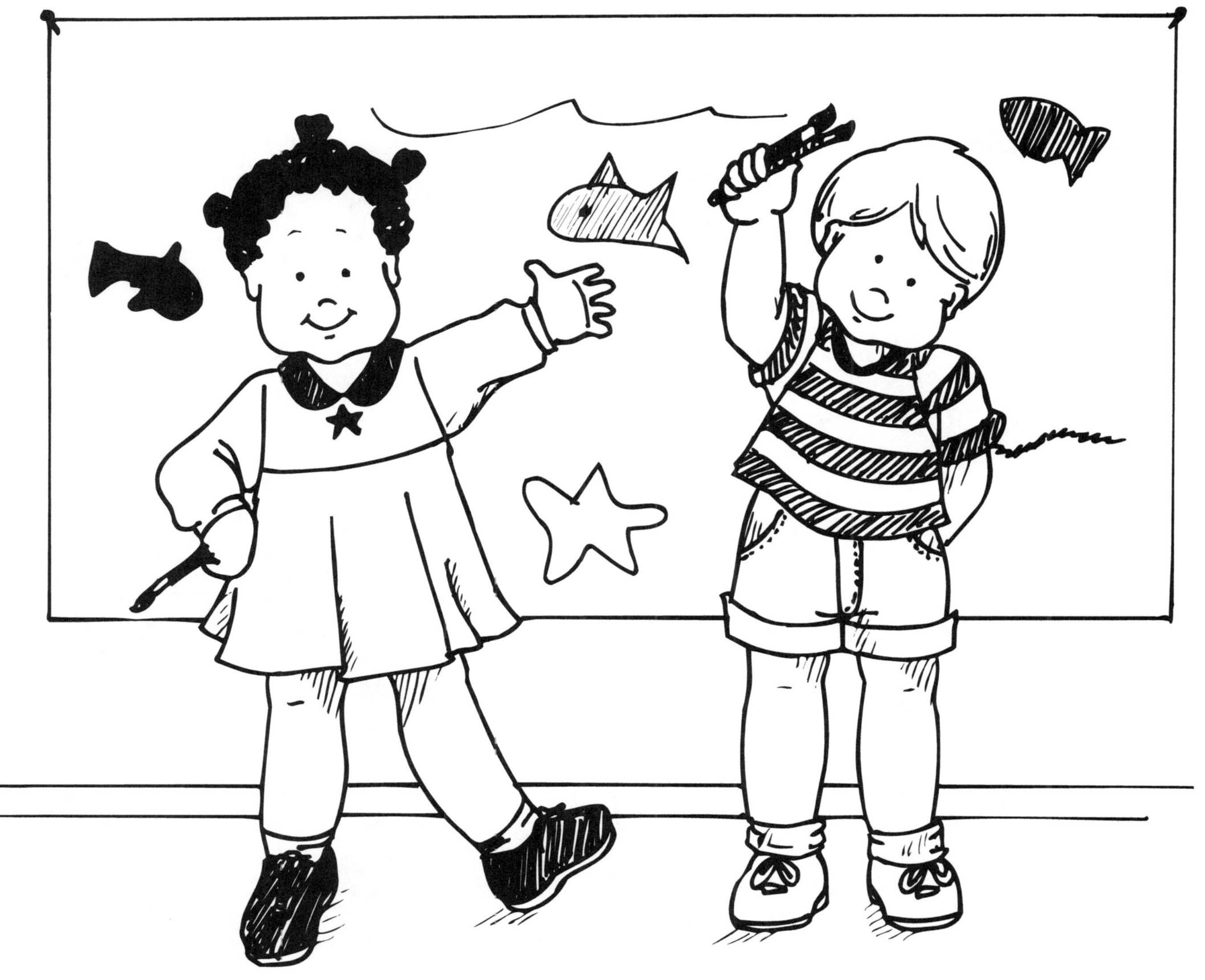

Painting

Swirling Colors

Set out many different colors of paint in plastic squeeze bottles. Give the children a variety of different types of paper to work with (paper plates, large sheets of easel paper, construction paper, etc.) and different sizes of paintbrushes. Encourage the children to mix the paints to create new colors. Ask them what they might name a brand new color. Show them some examples of different colors and read them the color names of crayons. This will help stretch their imaginations. Hang their new colors up. You can encourage the children to print their names, and you can help them write the names of their new colors.

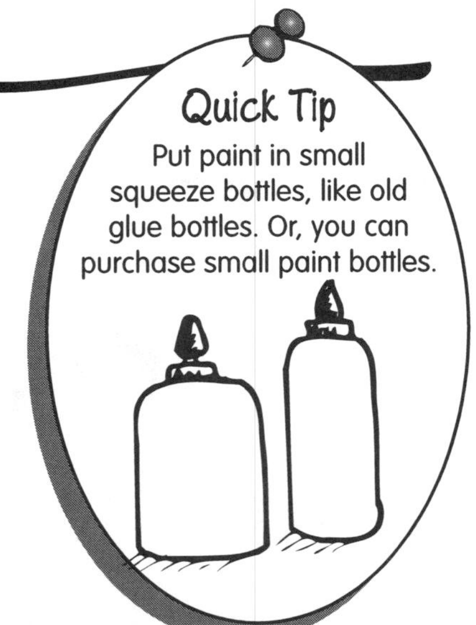

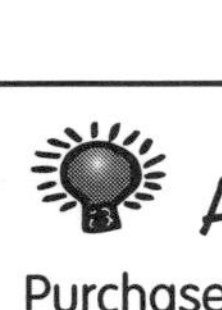

Another Idea

Purchase or ask parents for food flavoring, such as lemon, vanilla, mint, etc., to add to paint. Let the children paint vanilla white pictures, green mint pictures, and yellow lemon pictures. Encourage them to mix the scents and colors together to see what they create. Hang their creations for all to see.

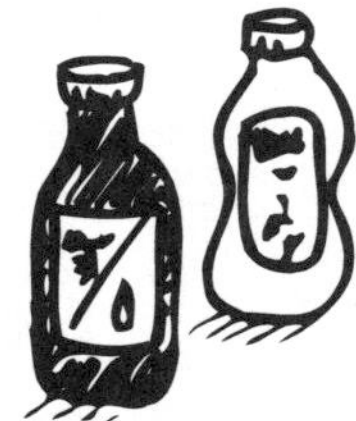

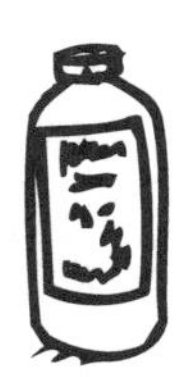

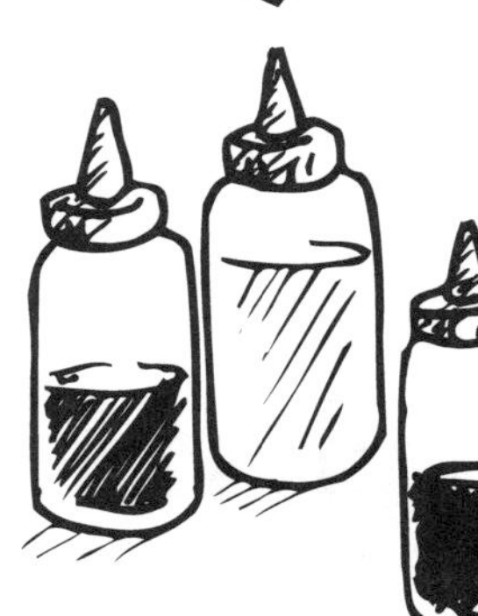

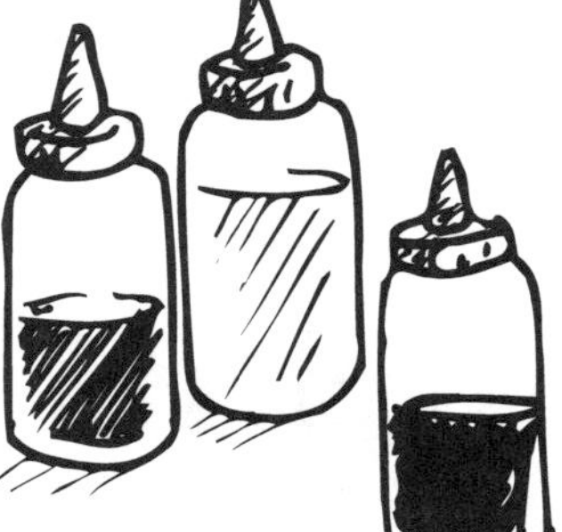

Dabbling in Cotton

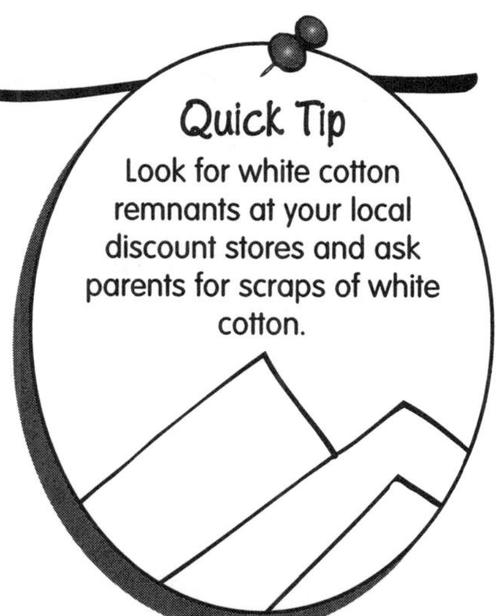

Explain to the children how cotton grows and show them a picture of cotton or a cotton plant. Next, let them feel cotton balls and cotton products. Set out white cotton cloth in an area where all the children can work during the day. You can have many different sizes of remnants or just a few large ones. (Be sure to place newspaper under the cotton if you are not hanging it on a fence or easel.) Place some paint on foam trays or in bowls along with a variety of brushes. Encourage the children to paint the cotton, creating a wonderful fabric design. Next, hang the cotton murals up in the classroom or on a clothesline, inside or out.

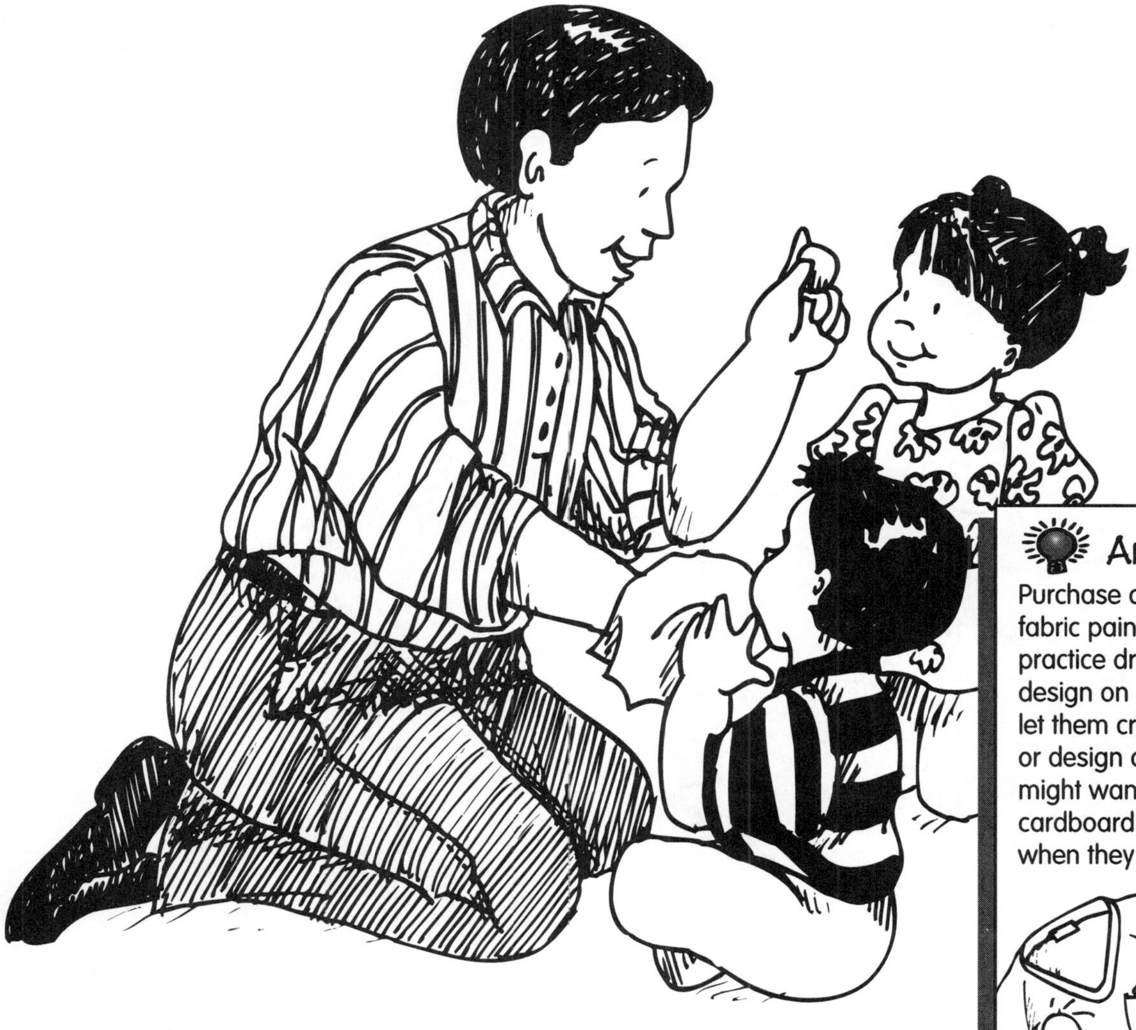

Another Idea

Purchase cotton T-shirts and fabric paint. Let the children practice drawing a picture or design on a piece of paper. Then let them create the same picture or design on their T-shirts. (You might want to put a piece of cardboard inside their shirts when they are painting on them.)

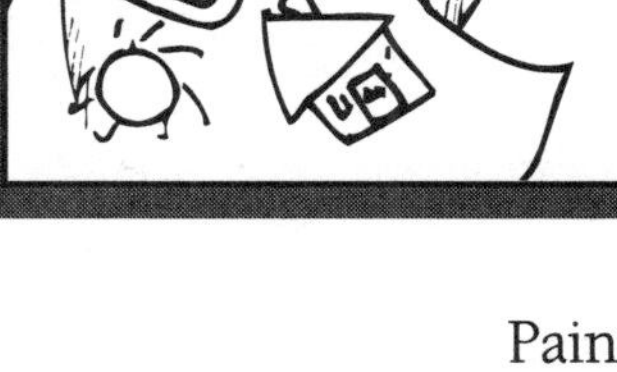

Shiny Tinsel Fun

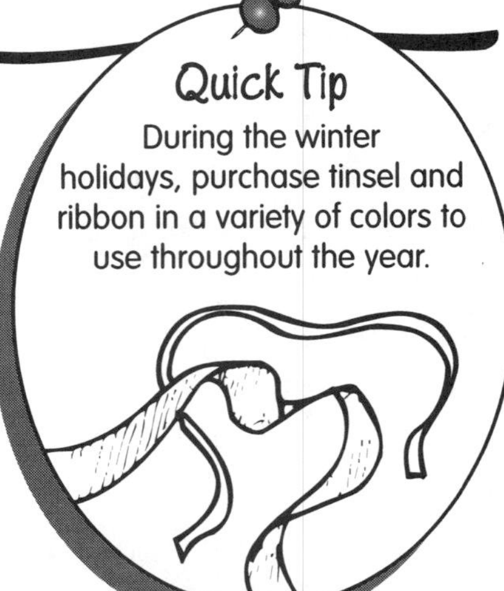

Cut a variety of different kinds of paper into shapes—triangles, circles, rectangles, hearts, etc. Make some shapes large and others small, along with many sizes in between, to give the children lots of choices.

Set out small amounts of paint in individual containers, paintbrushes, and the paper shapes you cut out. In separate containers, place tinsel and ribbon. Let the children paint pictures and incorporate tinsel and ribbon into their paintings. Show them how they can put paint on their shape papers, then ribbon and tinsel. Or, they can put ribbon or tinsel on first and then paint over it. Encourage the children to try a mix of any and all of the combinations they can find.

Display the children's shiny tinsel creations in an area where parents can see and inquire about them. Show everyone how creative children can be in a creative classroom.

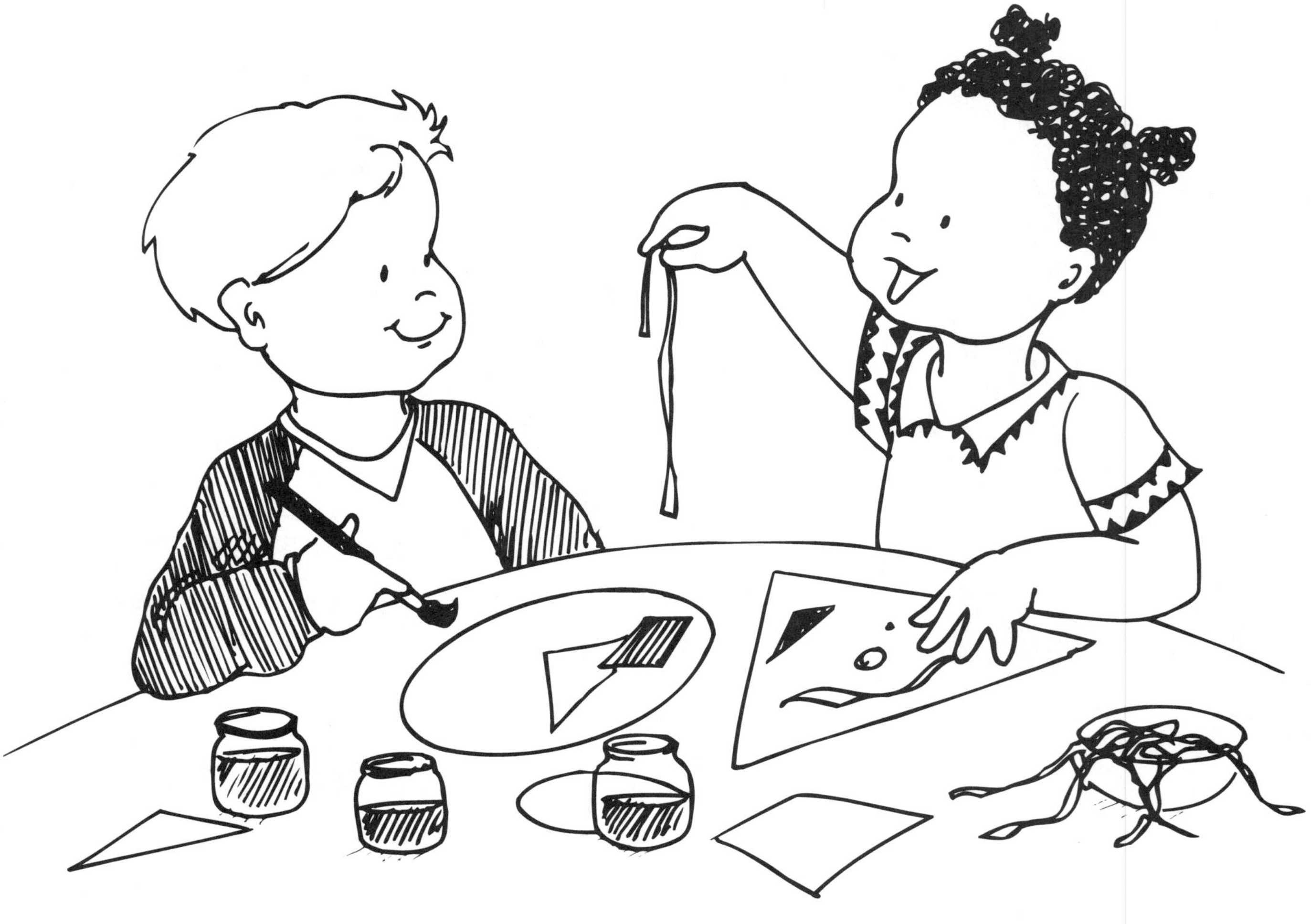

Together Is Better

Set aside enough long white sheets of paper (approximately 15 feet) so that you can place the children into groups. Gather a variety of paint, paintbrushes, and paint shirts. Hang the paper out on the playground wall or fence. Be sure there is enough space so that the children have elbow room. Gather the children together and divide them into groups.

Let each group know that part of this project is for them to talk about and decide what they want to paint together, such as a flower garden, an ocean, a rainbow, etc. Next, show them where they will paint and give them the tools they need. As the children continue to work, set out other items they can add to their murals, such as tissue paper, glitter, etc. When the children are done, hang the murals in the eating area to share with fellow students, or hang them outside to share with their parents.

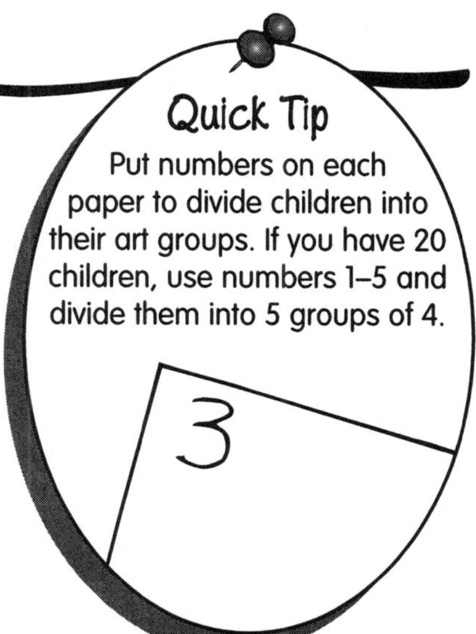

Another Idea

Cut large sheets of paper into circles and number each one. Cut enough so that each group of 3–4 children has one. Lay the paper circles out on the playground along with paint and paintbrushes. Divide the children into small groups and give each group a number. Have each group find its number on its circle. Next, let the groups paint their circles with pictures, patterns, or other designs. Hang the circle art from the ceiling and enjoy the view.

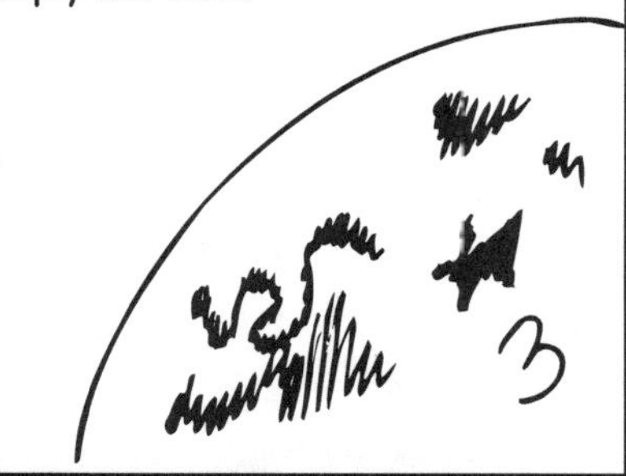

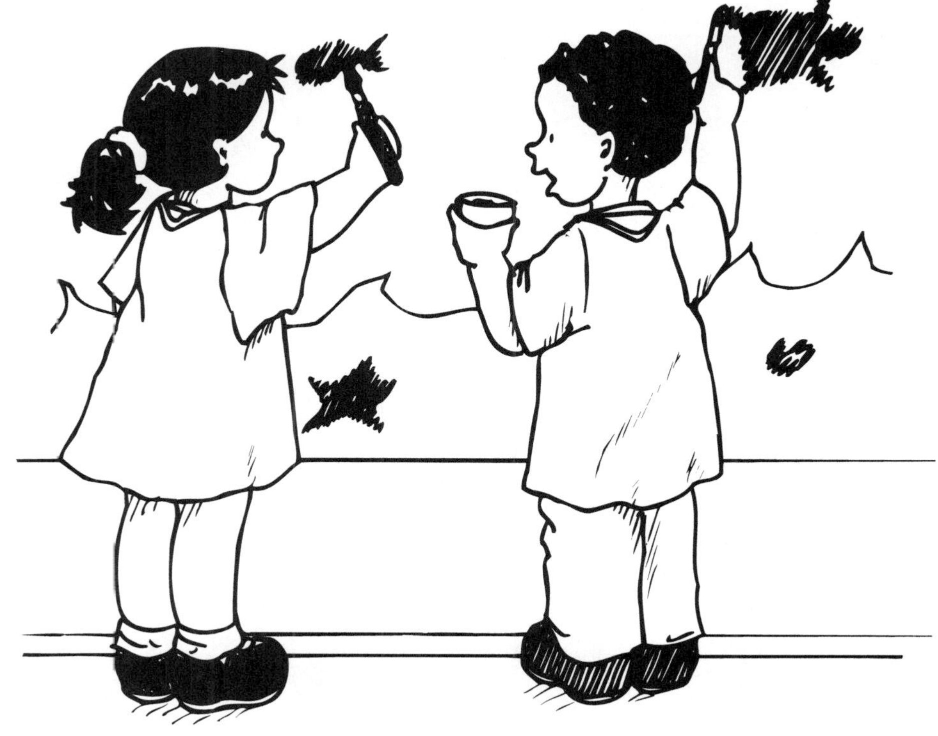

Glitter Glitz

Provide each child with a paint shirt. For this activity, prepare many different colors of glitter and paint. (See recipe to the right.) Cut paper into a variety of different shapes and sizes. Set the glitter paint and paintbrushes in the art area, and encourage the children to paint designs, pictures, and textures on their papers. When their creations are dry, hang them on a clothesline outside the room entrance for everyone to see. Be sure the children's names are on their artwork.

Quick Tip

Try this easy recipe:

Glitter Paint

spoonful of glitter
(You can use two colors to create a different look.)
1/3 cup paint
Mix well.

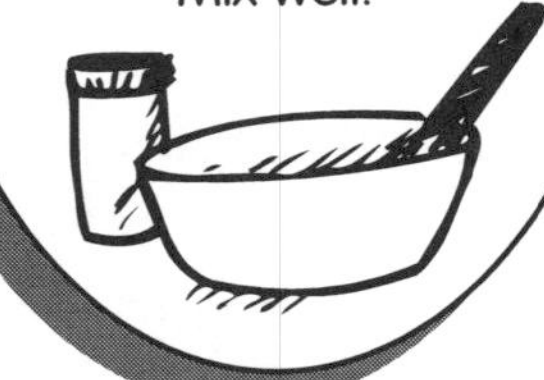

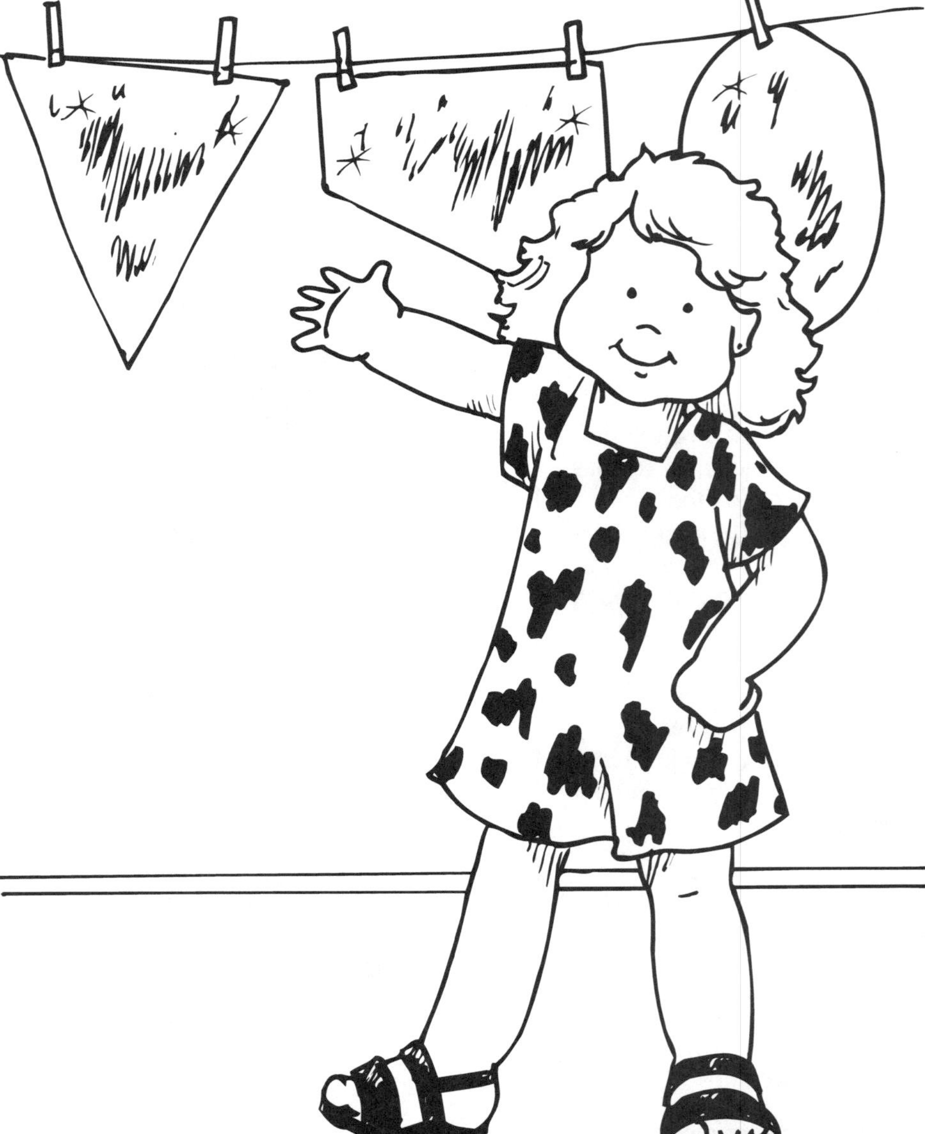

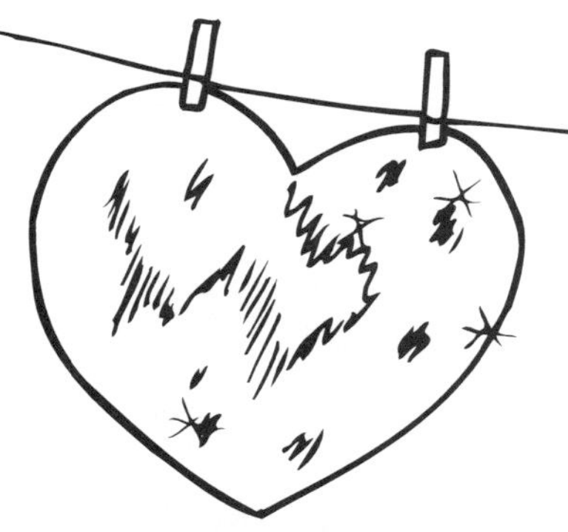

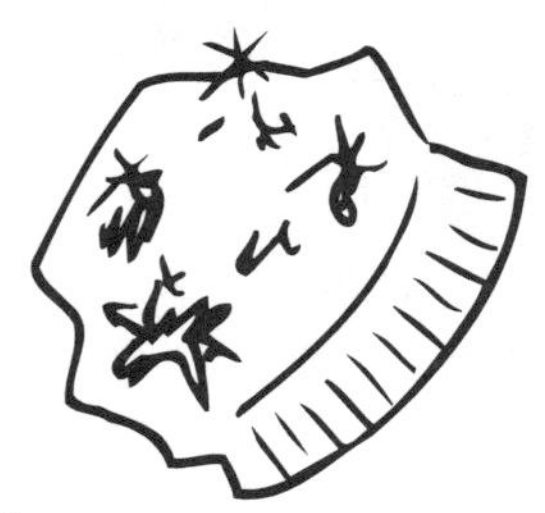

Another Idea

Set out paper plates, scissors, and glitter paint. Tell the children that they can cut the paper plates in a variety of ways. Demonstrate some cutting techniques. Next, let them cut and paint their plates. When they have finished, have each child print his or her name on a label and stick it onto the artwork. Send them home when dry for parents to hang up in a special place.

Tubular Fun

Purchase or ask parents for donations of colorful swim noodles. Use sharp scissors to cut them into various lengths, some very short, 1 to 8 inches, and others, 2 to 3 feet in length.

Set out large sheets of paper, and place different colors of paint in small plastic bowls. Set the bowls on foam trays. Set the noodles out next to the paint. Show the children how to dip one end or side of the noodle into the paint and then move or roll the noodle around on the paper, coming up with some unique designs. (Each noodle will produce somewhat of a different design because of its size.) The children can use different pressure with longer ones than shorter ones. It's fun to watch all the motion and creative energy that comes with tubular fun. After the paintings dry, attach them to a long, clean noodle and display them by hanging the noodle up with string tied at both ends and the middle. Hang from the ceiling.

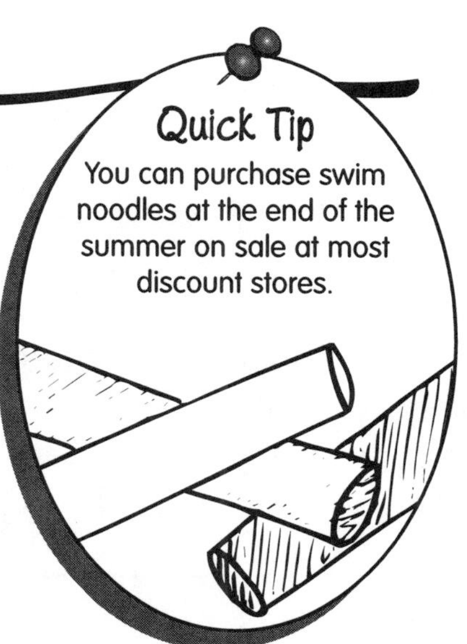

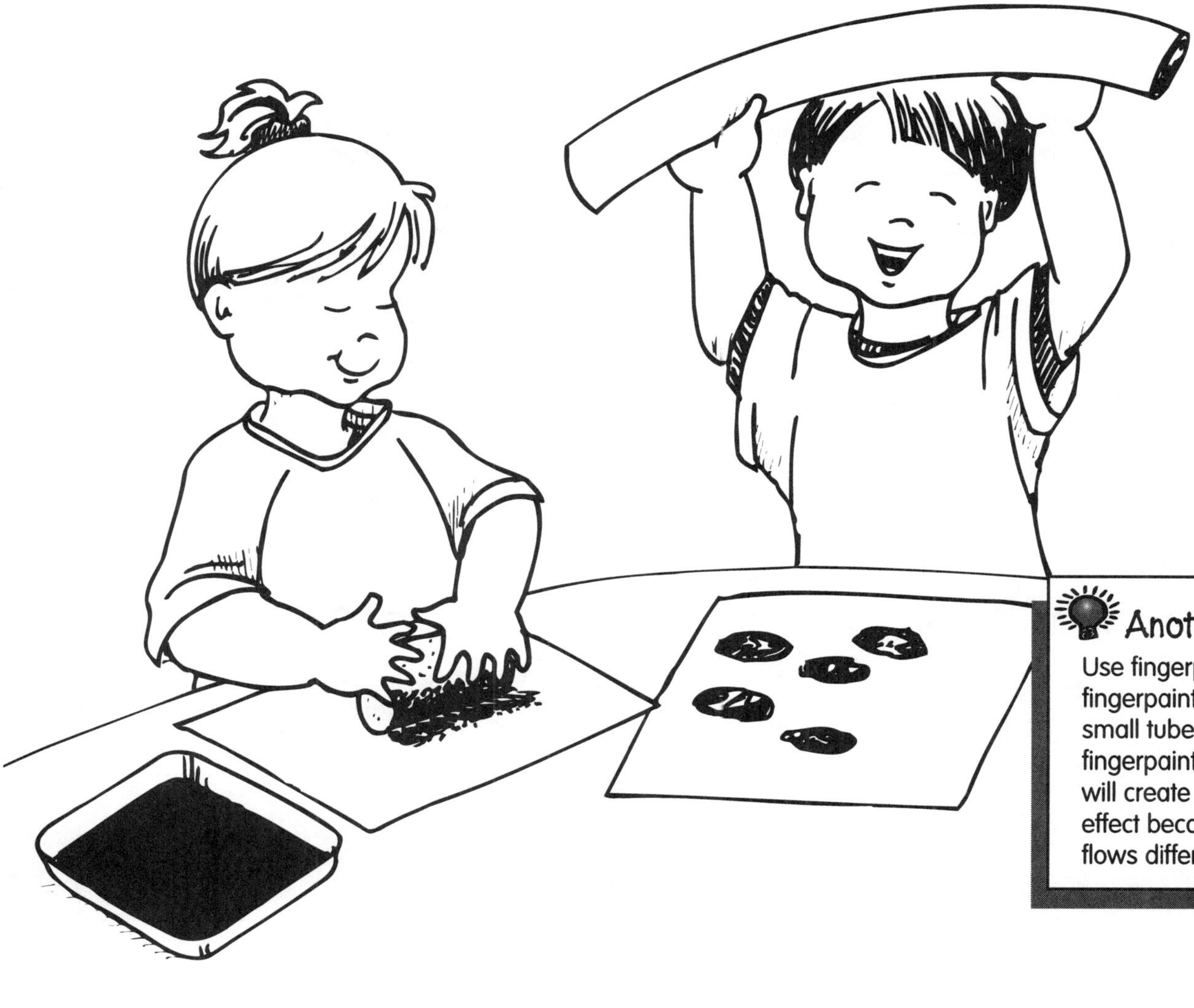

Another Idea

Use fingerpaint and fingerpaint paper with small tubes. The fingerpaint and paper will create a different effect because the paint flows differently.

Spin Painting

Find a variety of lids to cardboard boxes and a variety of tops. Put pieces of paper in the box lids. Divide the children into groups and let each group experiment with spinning the tops. As the children are practicing with the tops, set out small amounts of paint on foam trays. Give each group a few trays of paint. Encourage the children to dip the end of a top in paint, and spin it around in a cardboard lid. Have the children use different colors and tops to produce different results.

Quick Tip

Spinning tops come in a variety of shapes and sizes. You may want to start collecting them for science and art.

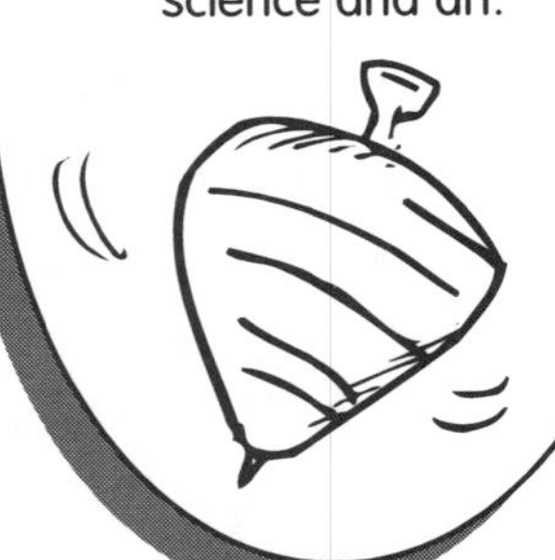

Another Idea

Let the children use golf balls that have been dipped in paint and roll them around in the box lids. The children can roll the balls in different colors and create fun designs. Hang them up all over the room to brighten the day.

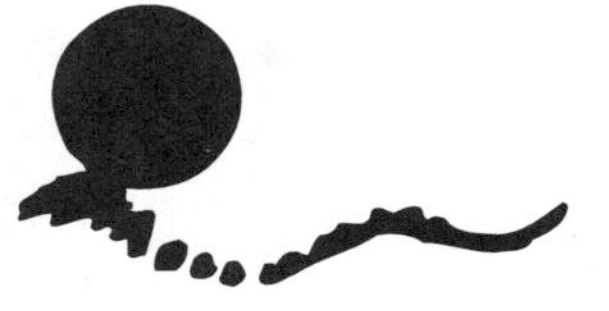

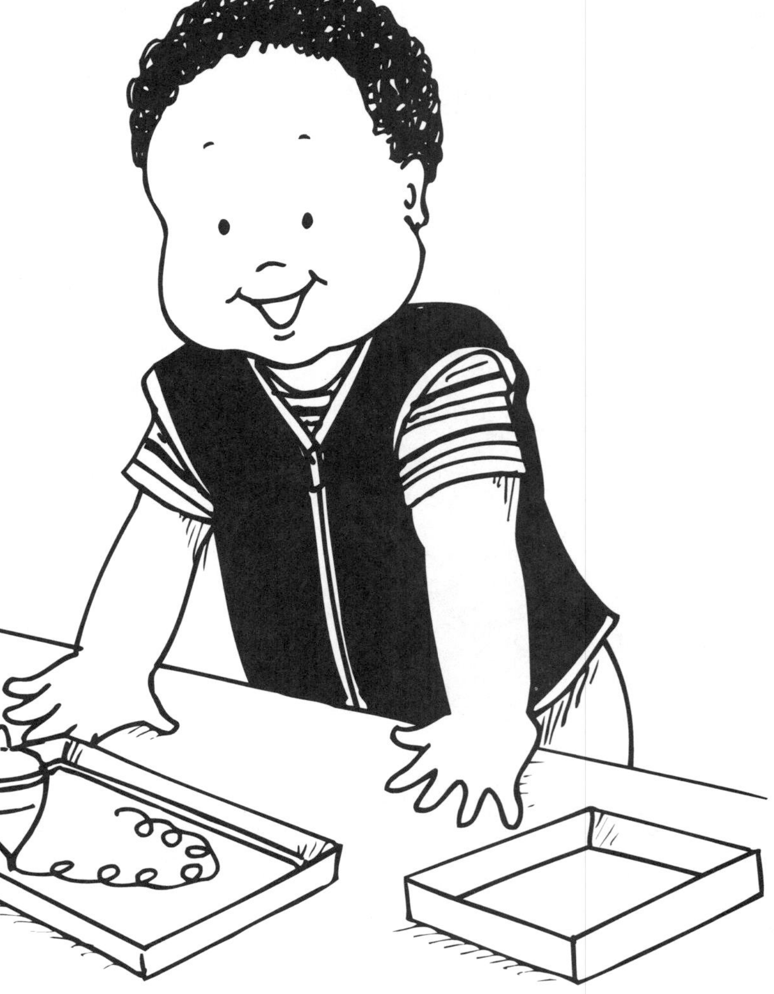

Spinning Wheels

Gather a variety of plastic vehicles having different sizes and textures of tires. Put about two tablespoons of paint on foam trays. Prepare a variety of colors. You can add glitter to some of the paint if you like. Cut long sheets of paper or use easel paper to provide plenty of room for the vehicles to move around. Set the paint, paper, and vehicles out on the playground or on tables in the art center for the children to do Spinning Wheels.

Show the children how to dip the wheels into the paint and move the vehicles across the paper. The children will begin to notice that the paint starts out going on thick and deep-colored and then gets lighter-colored. The children can make tracks of all sizes and textures using multiple colors of paint. When dry, set the prints up in an area where there is block play, or hang them up as a display called Spinning Wheels.

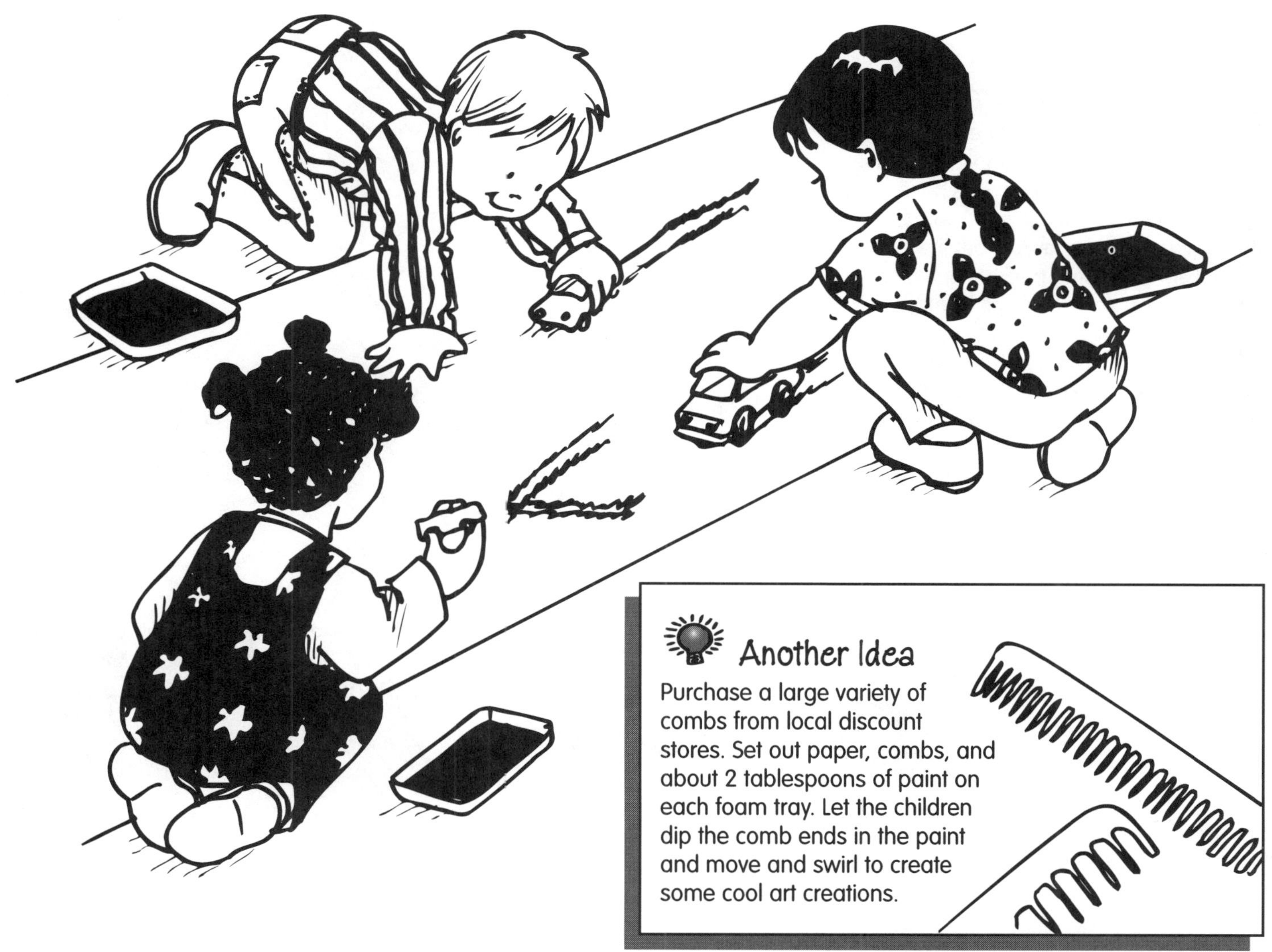

Another Idea

Purchase a large variety of combs from local discount stores. Set out paper, combs, and about 2 tablespoons of paint on each foam tray. Let the children dip the comb ends in the paint and move and swirl to create some cool art creations.

Paintbrush Mania

Set out several colors of paint, paper, paint shirts, and about 10 different paintbrushes for the children to choose from. Encourage the children to use the different paintbrushes in their paintings. They can discover wide, narrow, curved, etc., while doing Paintbrush Mania. The children will have the opportunity to create pictures differently when given a selection of brushes. Let dry and send home or hang in your classroom.

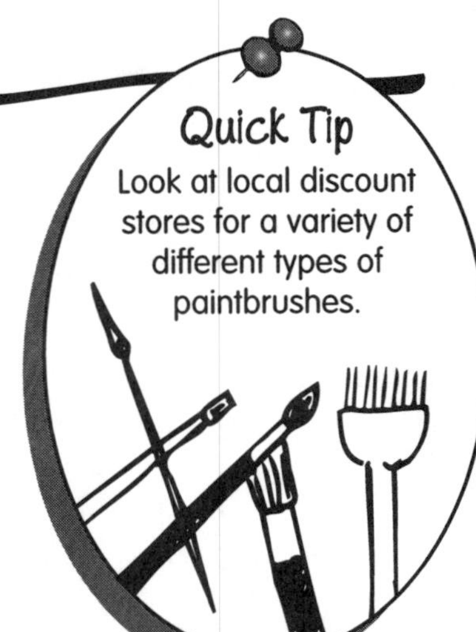

Quick Tip

Look at local discount stores for a variety of different types of paintbrushes.

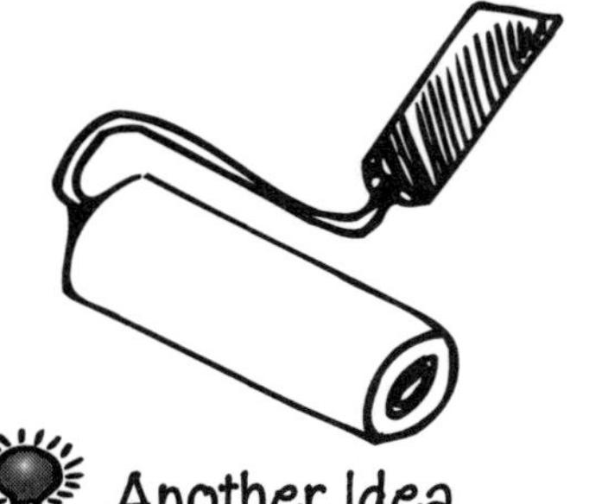

Another Idea

Ask your local paint store to donate a few affordable paint rollers to your school. You might also purchase some from local discount stores. On a warm sunny day, set out the paint rollers and some buckets of water that the paint rollers will fit into. Encourage the children to dip the rollers in the bucket and paint the sidewalks with designs. Ask the children what they would call their designs. Tell them to take a good look at their designs because they will disappear quickly.

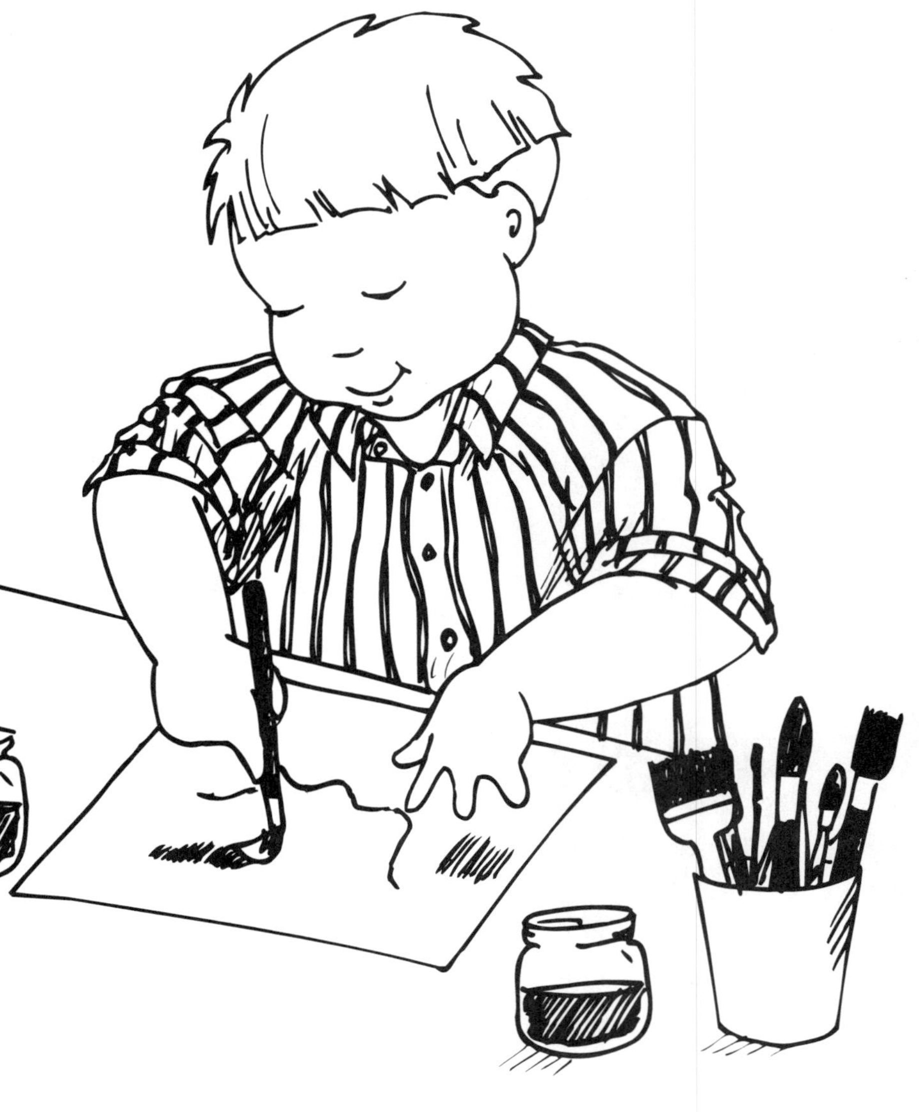

Textured Seed Paint

Ask the children what they think would happen if seeds were mixed with paint. Set out paint with seeds mixed in, paintbrushes, and paper for the children to use at an easel or art table. Be sure the children wear their paint shirts. Ask the children to describe the textures of their art creations and tell you about their seed painting experiences.

Quick Tip

Purchase birdseed and grass seed. Mix different colors of paint with the seeds to make a range of textures.

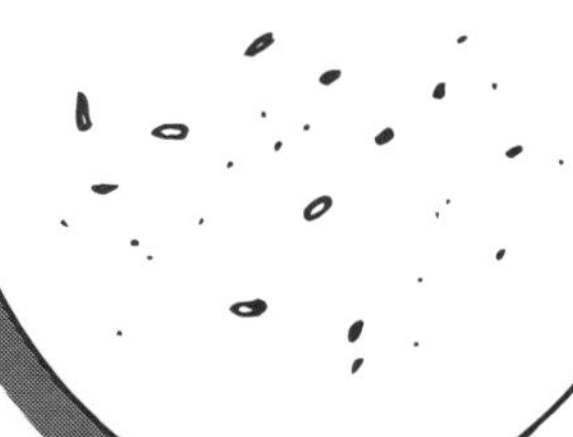

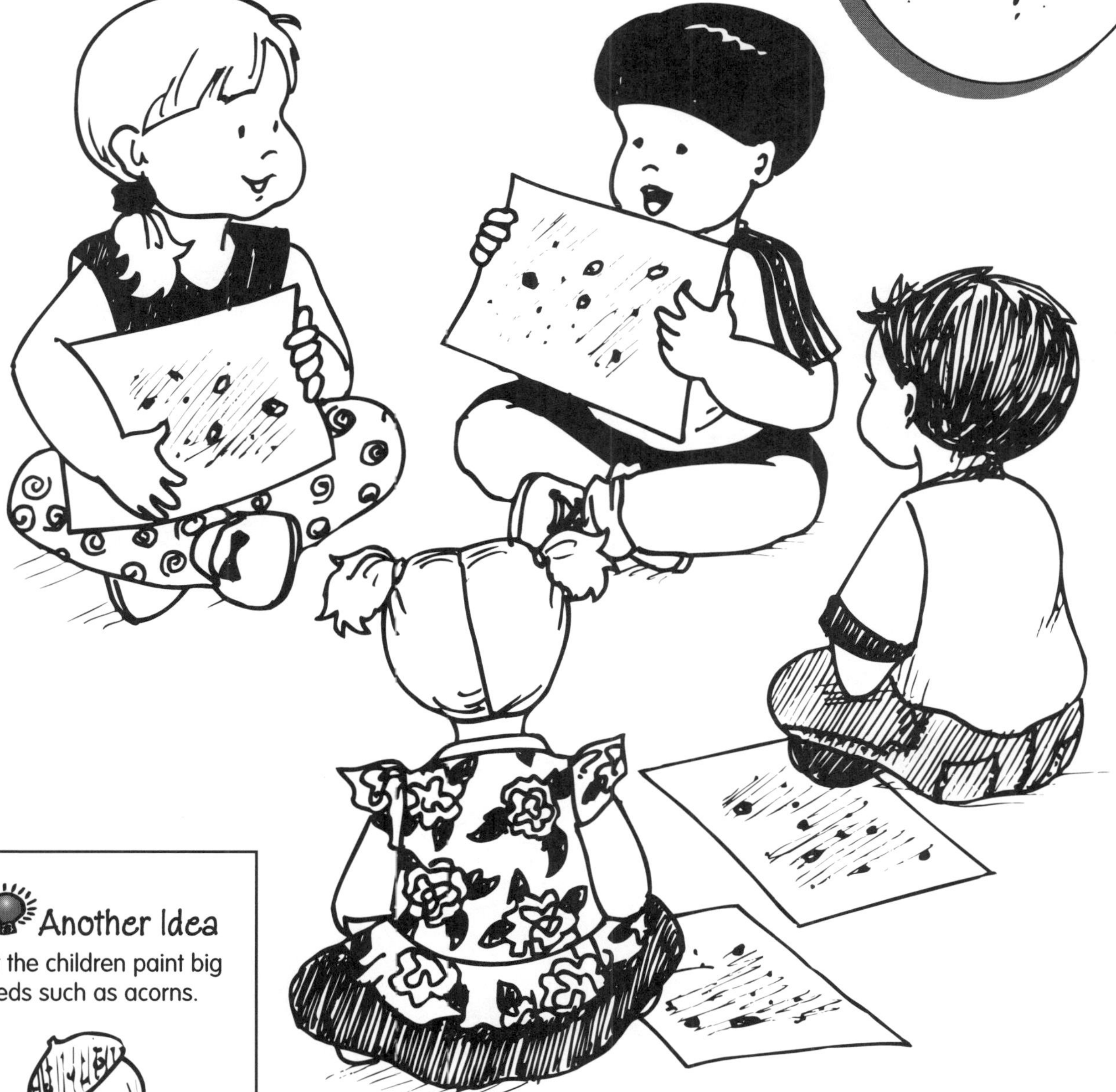

Another Idea

Let the children paint big seeds such as acorns.

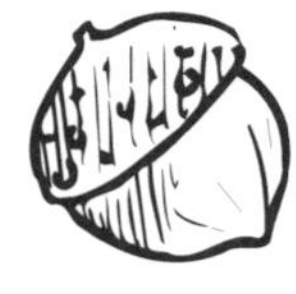

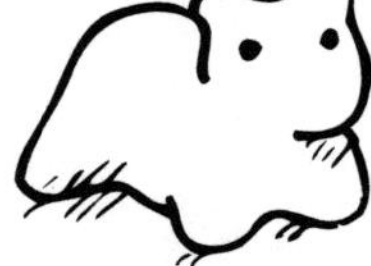

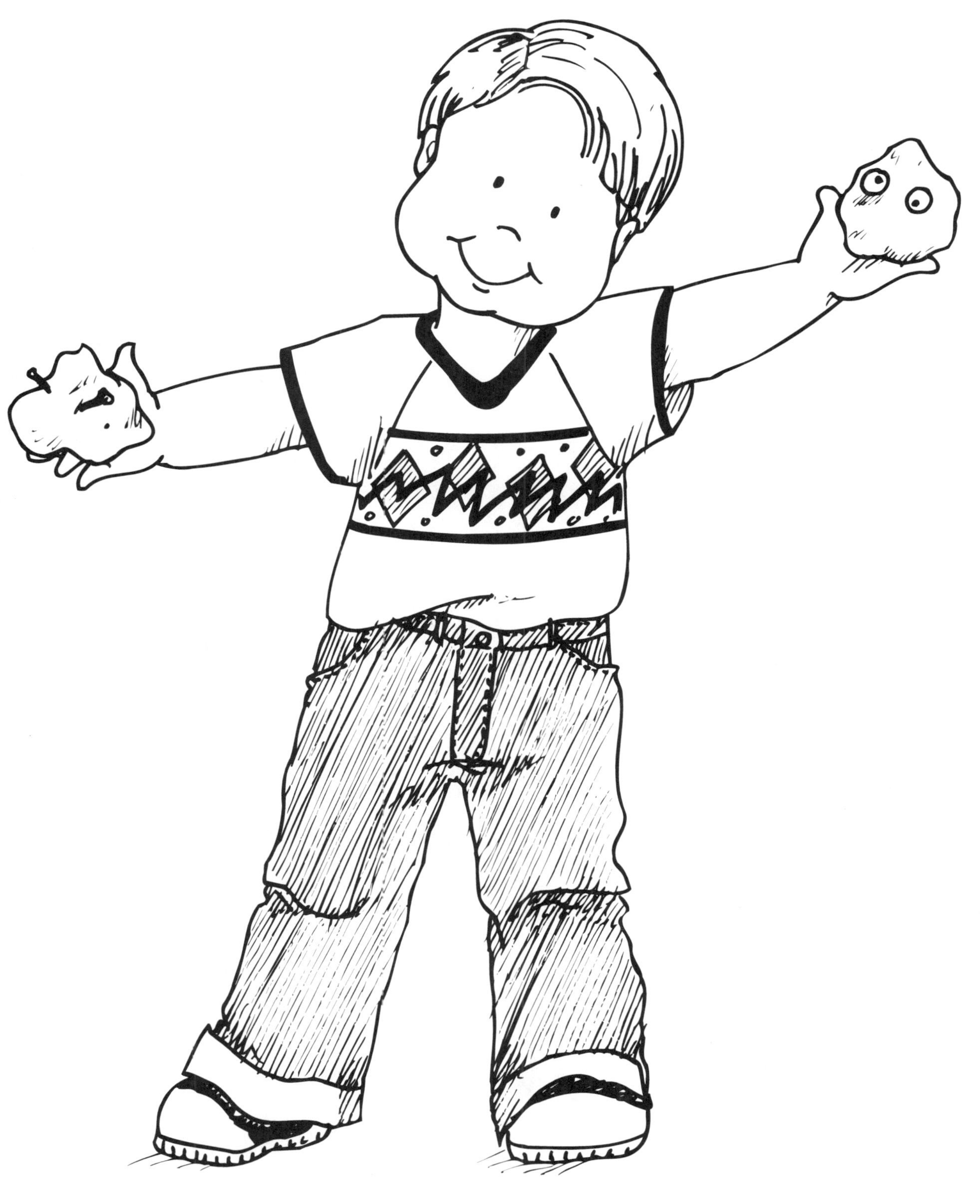

Sculpting

Aluminum Foil Designs

Purchase different thicknesses of aluminum foil and cut them into different sizes and lengths. Let the children roll the foil into different forms, such as long tubes, short tubes, balls of different sizes, etc. Next, encourage the children to twist and turn the foil into different shapes and figures. When finished, have each child prepare a name card using an index card. Display their creations along with their name cards in a designated area.

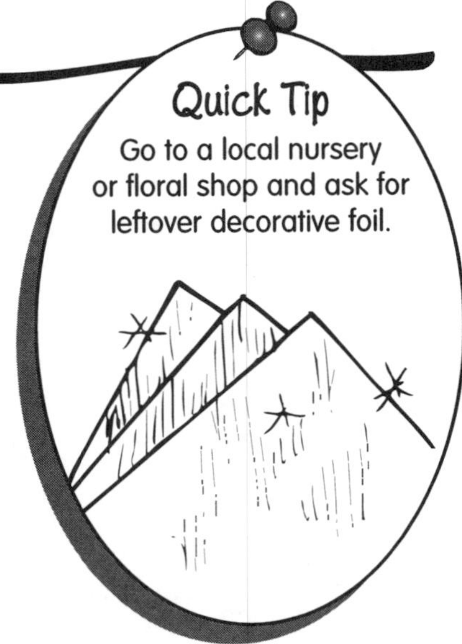

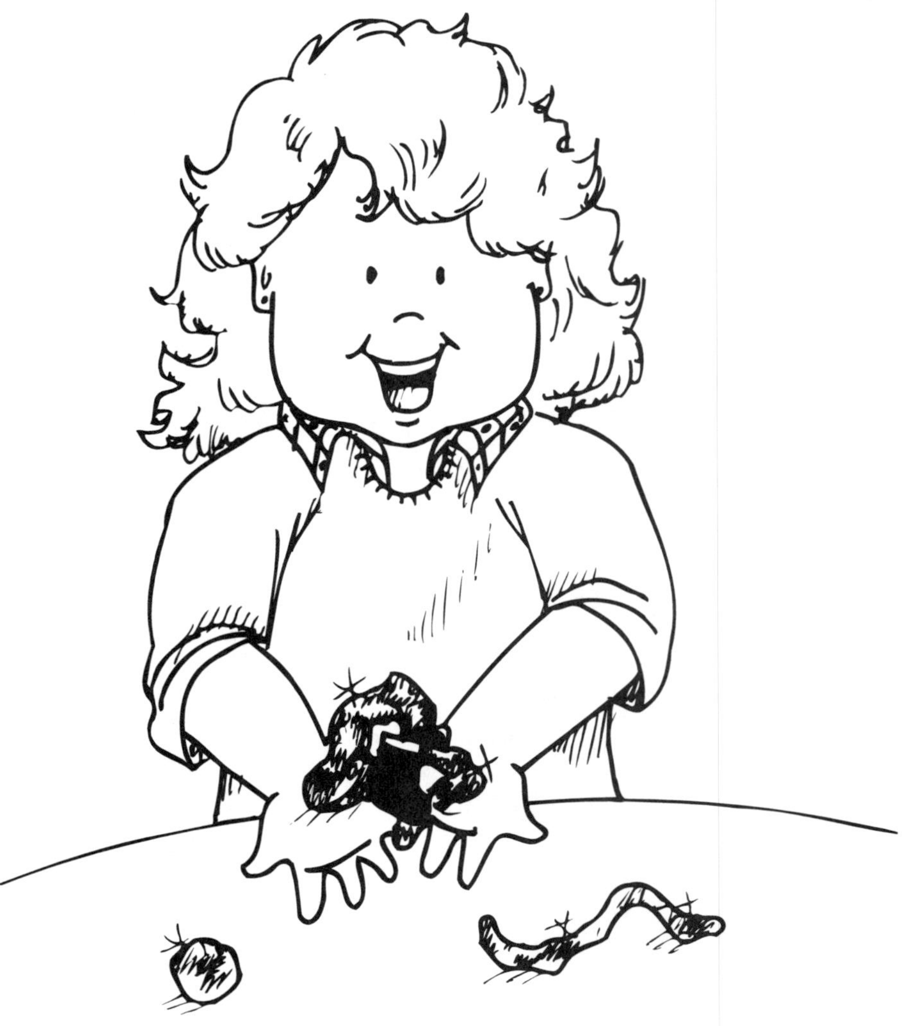

Another Idea

Pipe cleaners come in a variety of shapes, sizes, and colors. Set out a variety of pipe cleaners the children can use to create sculpture figures. Encourage the children to twist the pipe cleaners and then stick them into a clay stand or a Styrofoam base. Display them in your art gallery with the children's names attached, along with the name of each creation.

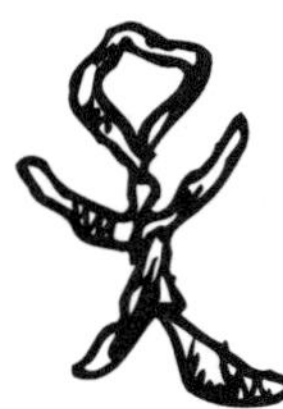

Wooly Creatures

Collect lint from your dryer and ask other staff members or parents to bring in their lint. Let the children look at all the different colors of lint and mix them together. Show them how to twist and turn the lint to create different shapes and forms. Let the children add sequins, glitter, and wiggly eyes to their creations. Give each child an envelope. Have the children write their names on the envelopes. When they are done with their wooly creations, they can stick them in their envelopes and take them home.

Quick Tip

Dry specific colors of clothing together to get that color of lint.

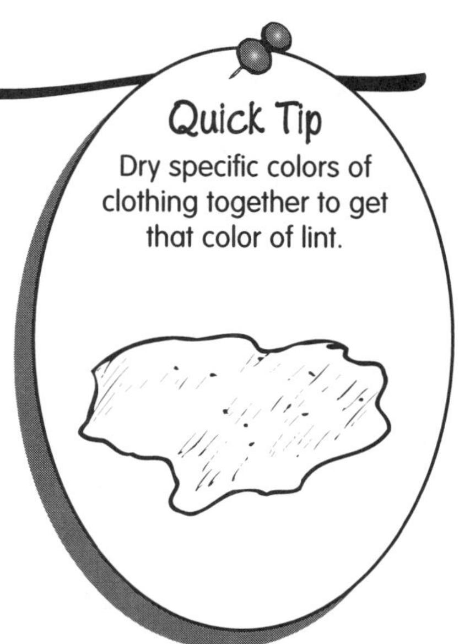

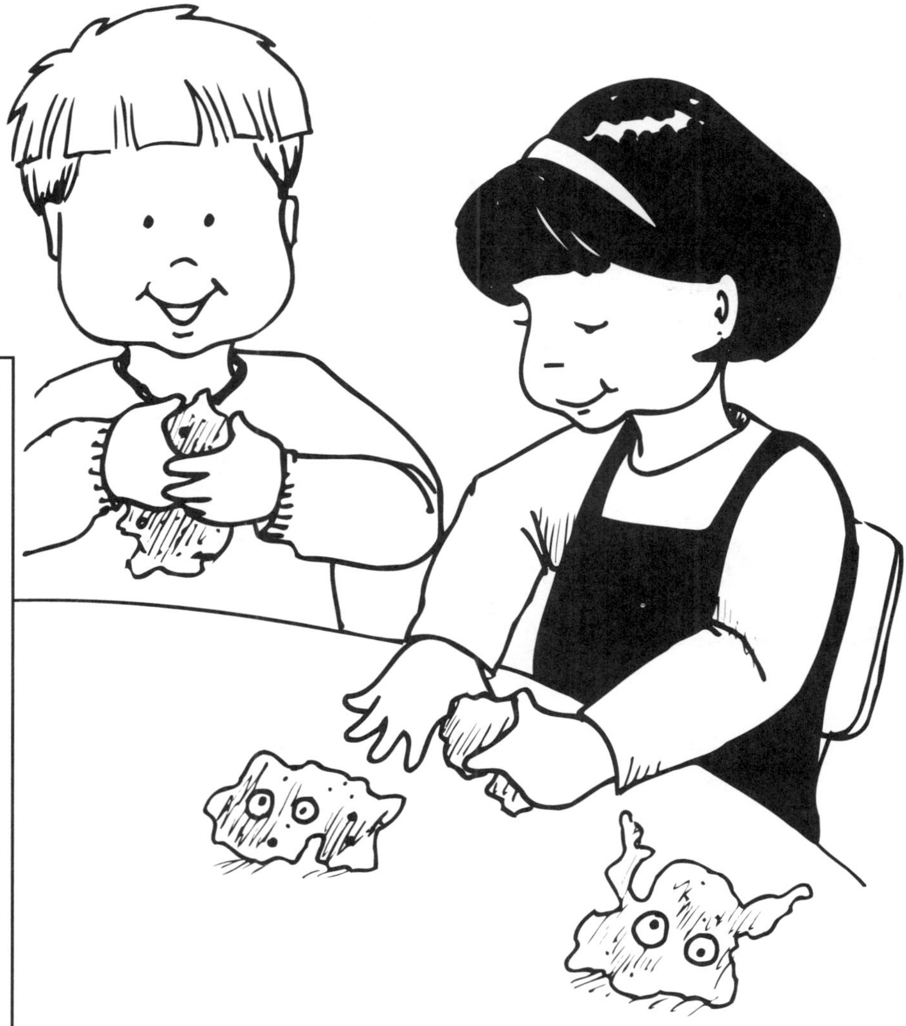

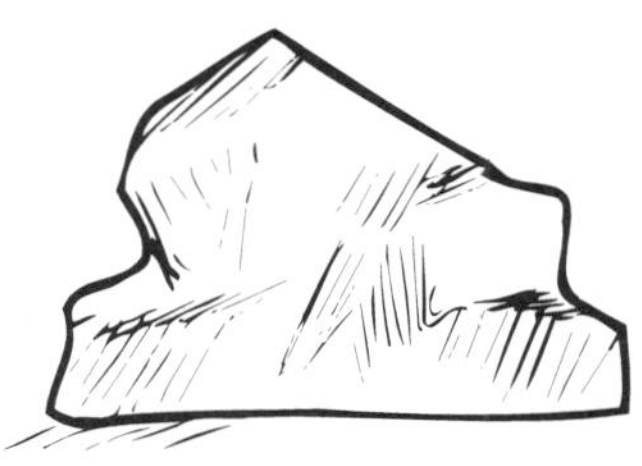

Another Idea

Follow the recipe on the back of Knox gelatin and add a small amount of food coloring. Place the gelatin in small plastic containers. Let it set in the refrigerator. Take the gelatin out of the plastic containers, and set it on trays along with a set of children's sculpting tools. Let the children sculpt away. (Sculpting tools can be purchased at local craft stores or through commercial catalogs.)

Sand Fantasies

Prepare some wet sand by mixing a small amount of water with dry sand until you have a consistency that keeps its shape. Set out the wet sand on a table or in large dishpans. Place sand, water, a misting bottle, and other sculpting tools, such as plastic hand shovels, rakes, craft sticks, etc., out for the children to use to create a range of sand sculptures. Show them what can happen when they sprinkle dry sand onto their wet creations.

You can also create colored sand for the children to use in their sculptures and add fish tank gravel to the sand for different textures.

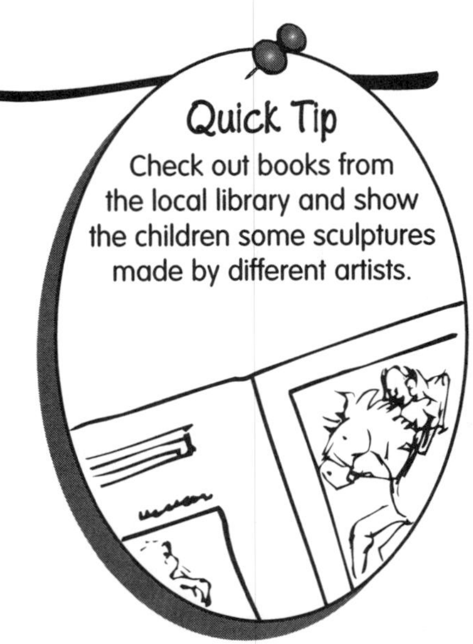

Quick Tip

Check out books from the local library and show the children some sculptures made by different artists.

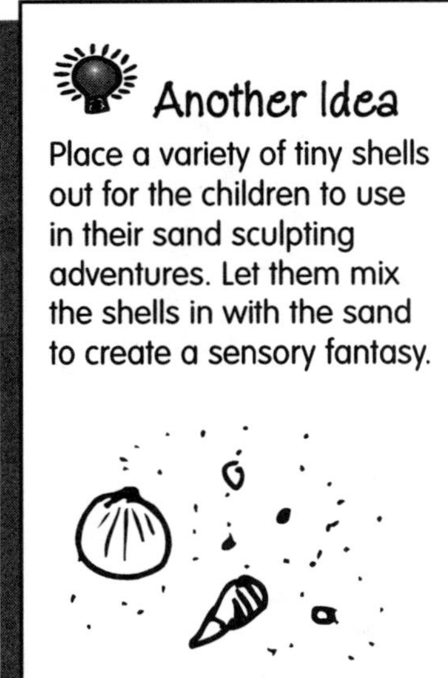

Another Idea

Place a variety of tiny shells out for the children to use in their sand sculpting adventures. Let them mix the shells in with the sand to create a sensory fantasy.

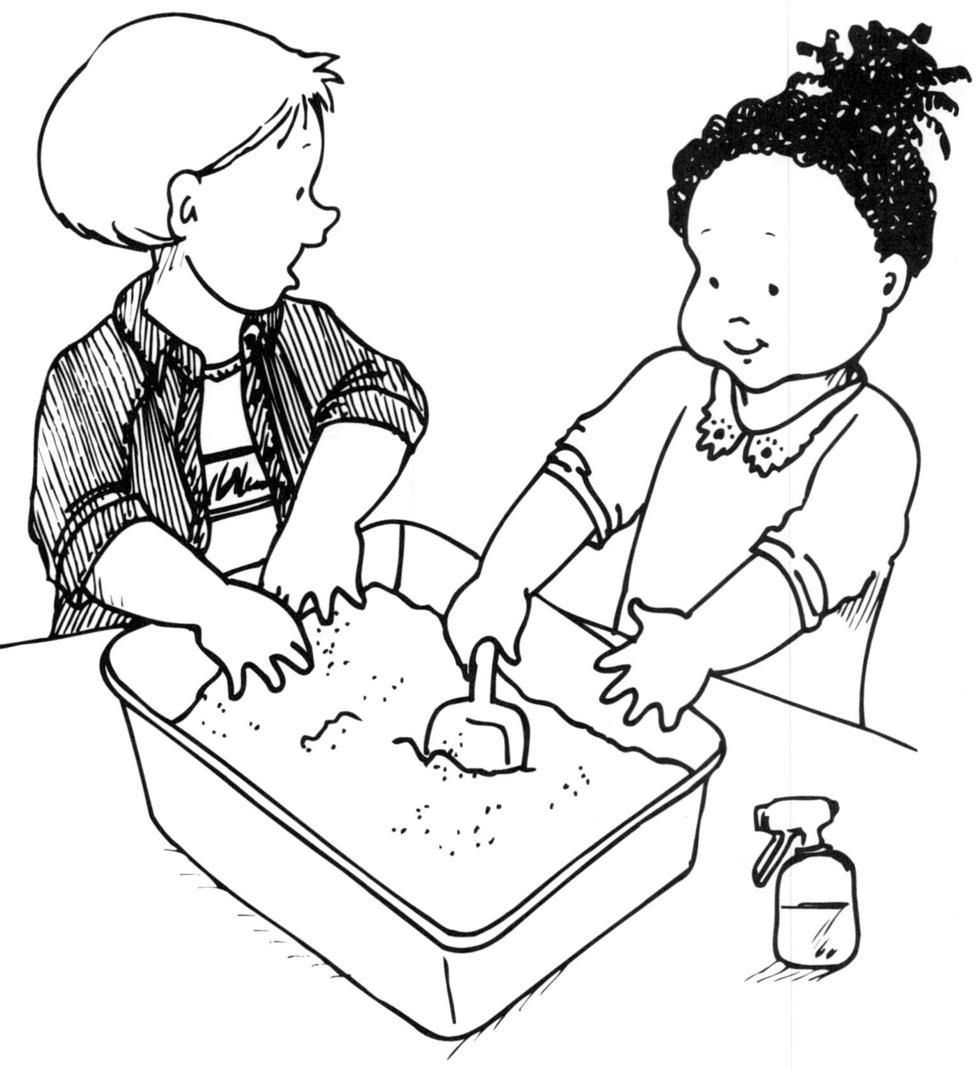

Creamy Creations

Set out bowls of various colors of shaving cream along with spoons, pipe cleaners, craft sticks, and toothpicks. Give each child a Styrofoam tray to create on. This way, when the children are finished, you can display their work on their trays. Encourage the children to form different sculptures out of the colorful selection of shaving cream. Show them how using craft sticks can add texture to their art forms. Let them stick pipe cleaners through the cream to see what happens. When they have finished, have the children wash their hands. Then they can take their foam trays to the designated area, and each child can make a name card to set next to his or her creamy creation.

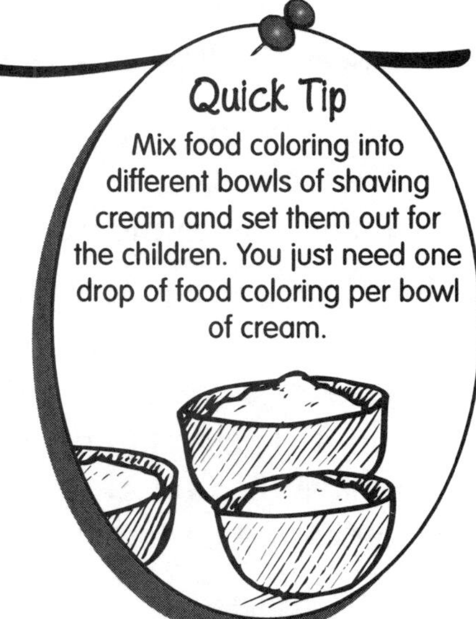

Quick Tip

Mix food coloring into different bowls of shaving cream and set them out for the children. You just need one drop of food coloring per bowl of cream.

Another Idea

Let the children sculpt with shaving cream and then use misting bottles to spray their sculptures.

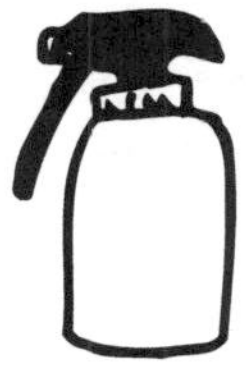

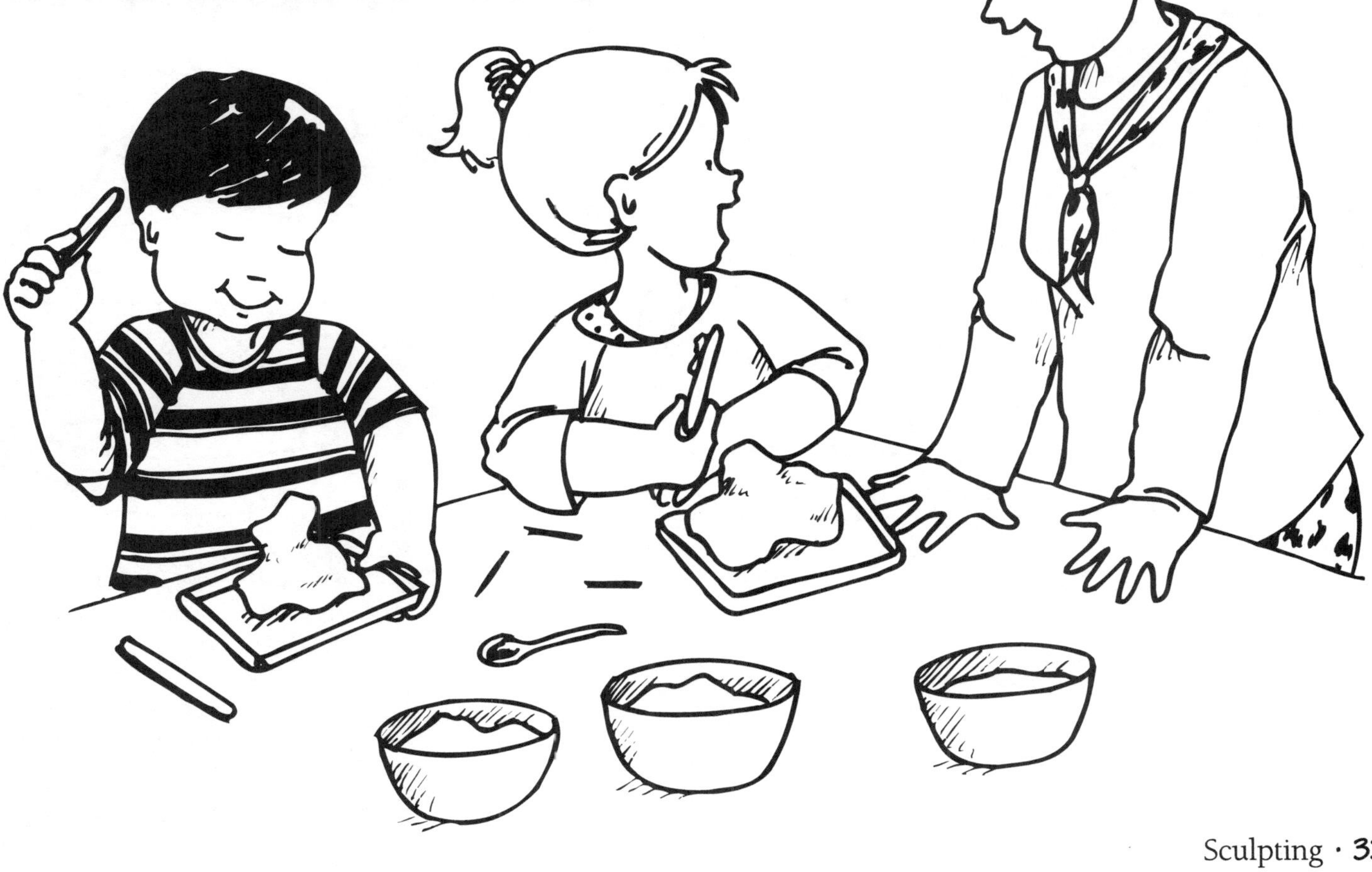

Icy Cold Concoctions

A few days before doing this activity, cut the tops off of juice and water bottles. Freeze water in these containers. Also make lots of ice cubes. (You can add food coloring to the water if you want to make colored ice for the children.)

To begin the activity, set out water bottles filled with water and misting bottles filled with water. Set the activity up on tables or in fluid tubs. Next, show the children how ice will melt and change forms when it is misted or when water is poured on it. The children will see the form change right before their eyes. Next, let them have the opportunity to sculpt the ice using the misting bottles and water bottles. When they have finished, their creations will melt away.

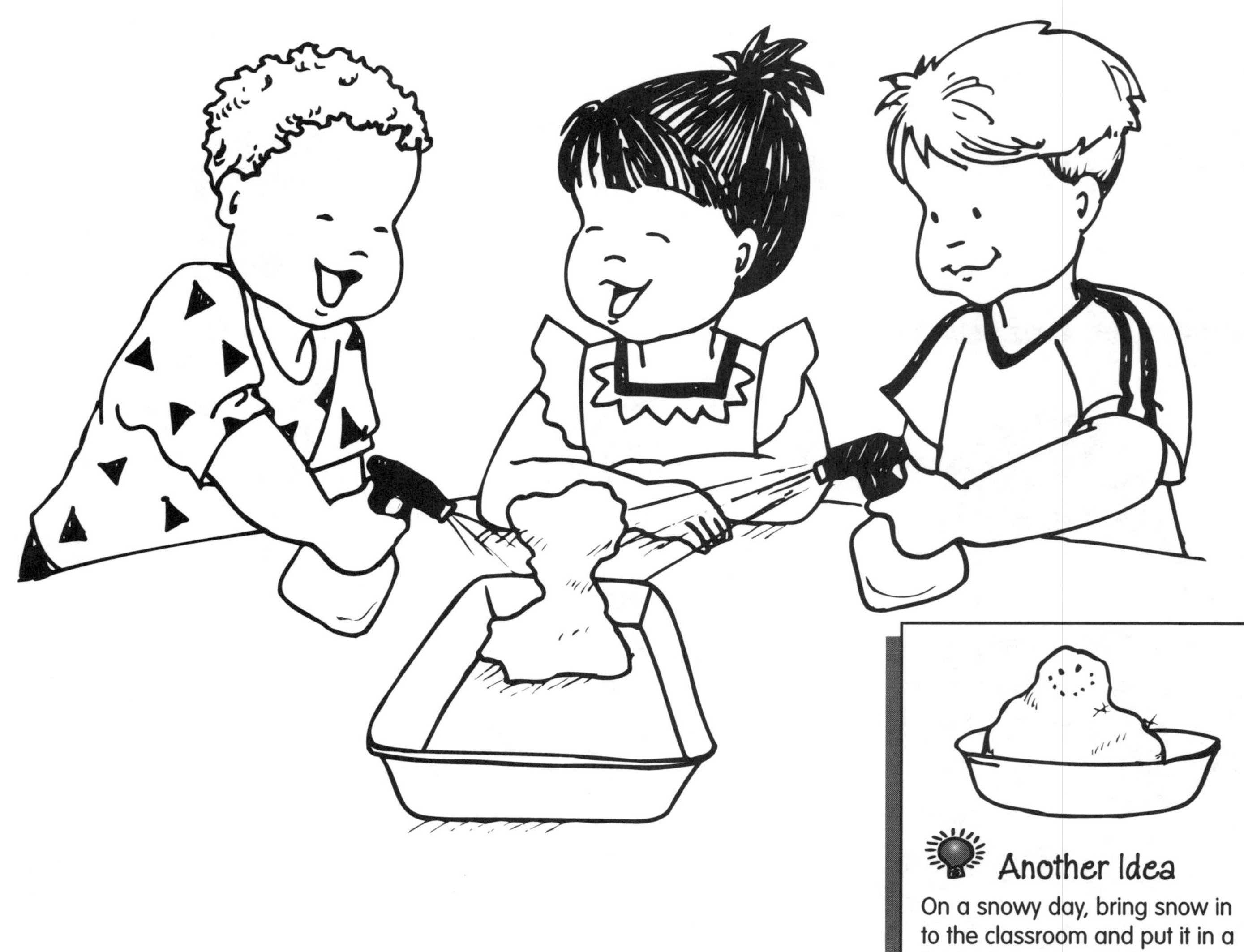

Another Idea

On a snowy day, bring snow in to the classroom and put it in a fluid tub. Let the children create with snow. You can add flavoring and/or food coloring to enhance this sculpting experience.

Earth Fun

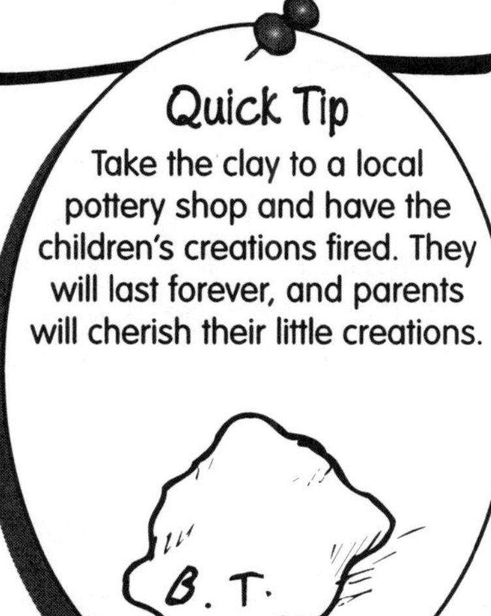

Quick Tip

Take the clay to a local pottery shop and have the children's creations fired. They will last forever, and parents will cherish their little creations.

Purchase a block of potters clay.* Break it up into equal parts so that each child in your class can have at least one chunk of clay. Set out bowls of water or a tub of water and paper towels. Find an area outside that is conducive to this rather messy activity.

Set out the clay and water where the children can reach it with little stress. Put smocks on the children. Show them how to dip their hands in the water just to moisten them. Next, without drying their hands, tell them to pick up their clay and begin to squish and work the clay with their hands. Let the children dip their hands in water as they feel their clay begin to dry out. Encourage them to be creative by using their hands to form the clay into different shapes or creations.

When the children are finished, help them carve their initials in their work with a pencil. Set their creations on newspaper in the sun to dry. Display them or send them home when dry.

*It is best to use potters clay outside because children will need to dip their hands in water to get the full effect of working with this medium.

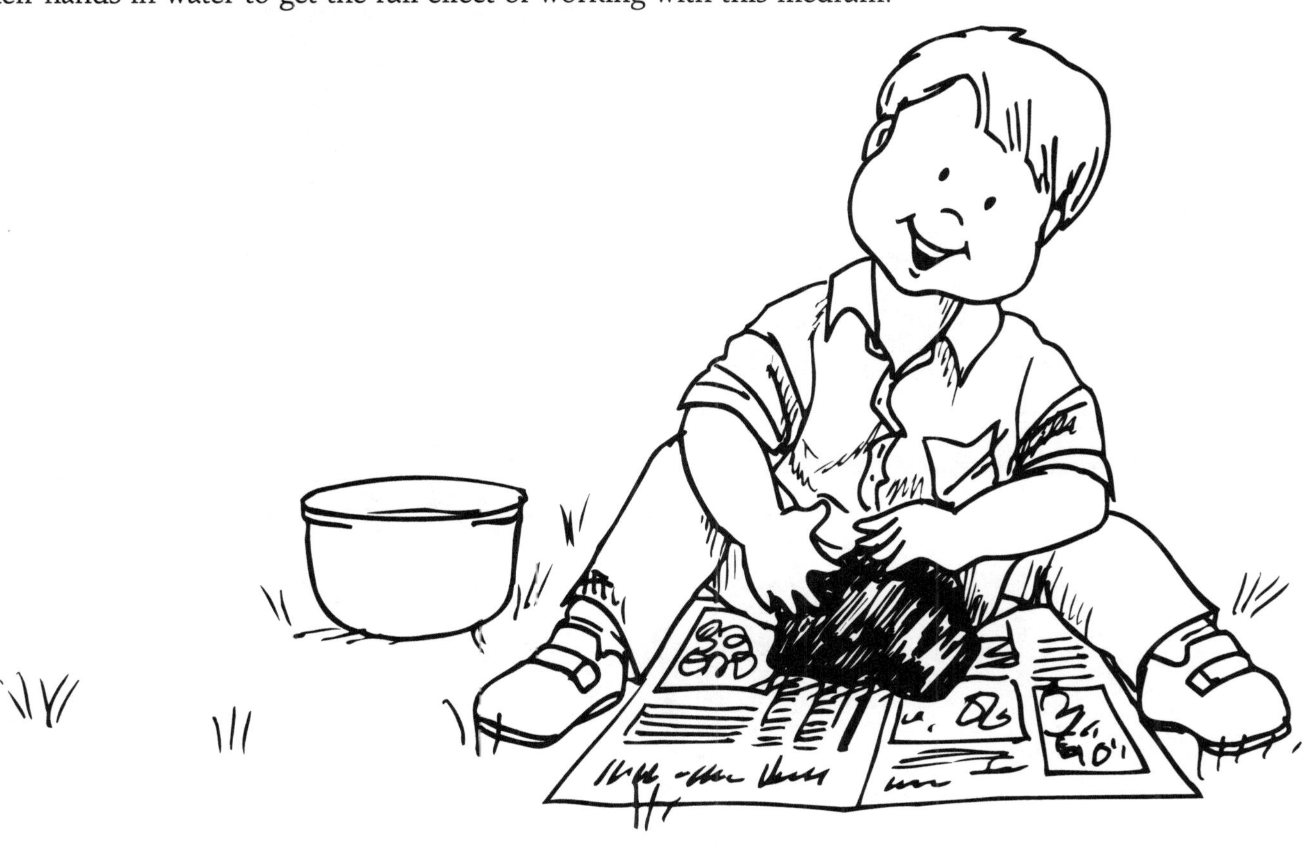

Clay Exploration

Prepare lots of clay (see recipe below) and place it in a plastic container with a lid. Set the clay out and let the children play with it. Encourage them to look at the texture and describe how it looks and feels. Next, have the children roll some of the clay into a ball. Give each child a clay hammer. Encourage them to pound the clay and put impressions in the clay with the hammer. Provide other materials for the children to hammer into the clay such as golf tees, poker chips, and golf balls.

When they have finished their work, ask the children to take all the objects out of the clay and see what it looks like. Then let them decide if they would like to display their pieces or roll them back into balls. If they roll them into balls, place the clay back in the container. If they wish to display their work, have them set them in an area and make name cards to put next to them. Name cards can be made using folded index cards.

Another Idea

Let the children add other ingredients to the clay such as a teaspoon of glitter, a teaspoon of sequins, or perhaps a teaspoon of coffee. Encourage them to mix their choice of ingredients in by molding the clay with their hands. Then they can create whatever comes into their imaginative little minds.

Sawdust Clay

3 cups flour

2 cups sawdust

1 cup salt

Mix the three ingredients together. Add water as needed to form a soft dough.

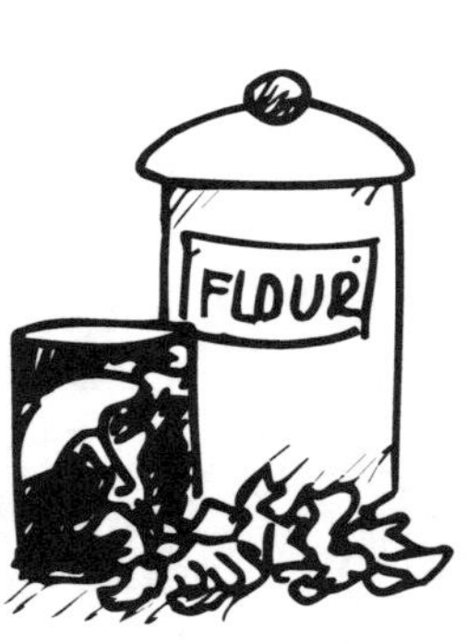

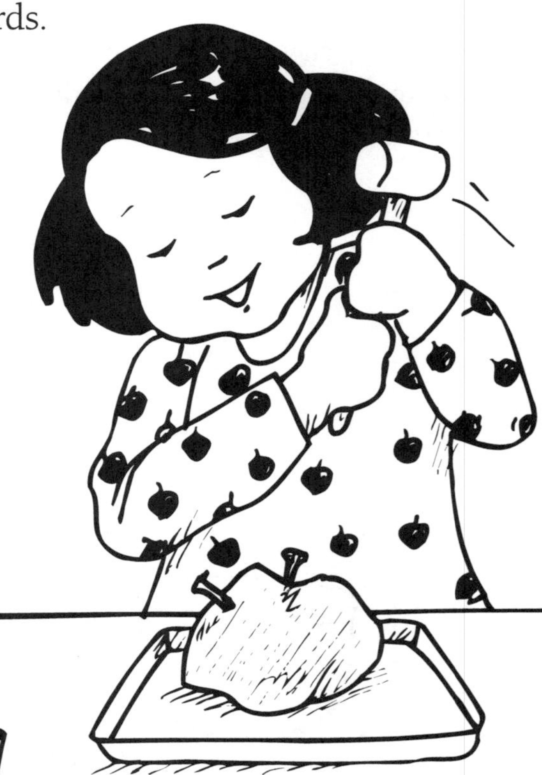

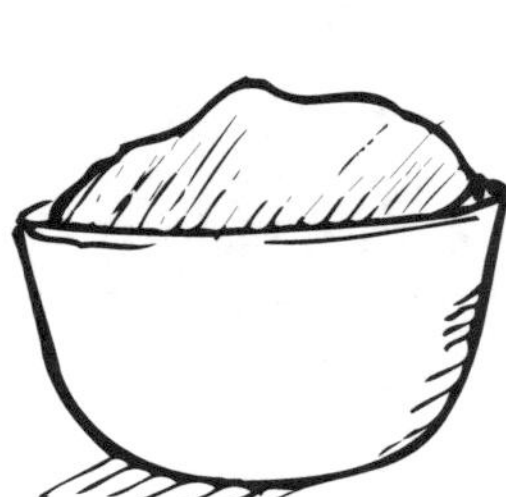

Sensory Fun

Set play dough (see recipe below) out on a table or individual trays. Let the children explore the play dough through touch, sight, and smell. Encourage them to create round balls that can be turned into people, animals, or beads. Show them how to roll a small ball out into a long snake and then coil it up. Give them cookie cutters to make shapes, or just let them create open-ended art.

When they have finished, have the children print their names on index cards or pieces of paper. Display them in an area where others can marvel at their work.

Quick Tip

Prepare the play dough the day before you do the activity and be sure to make plenty. Store in resealable plastic bags.

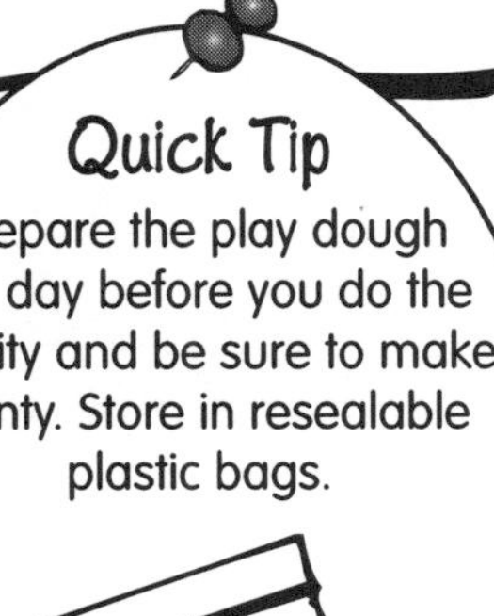

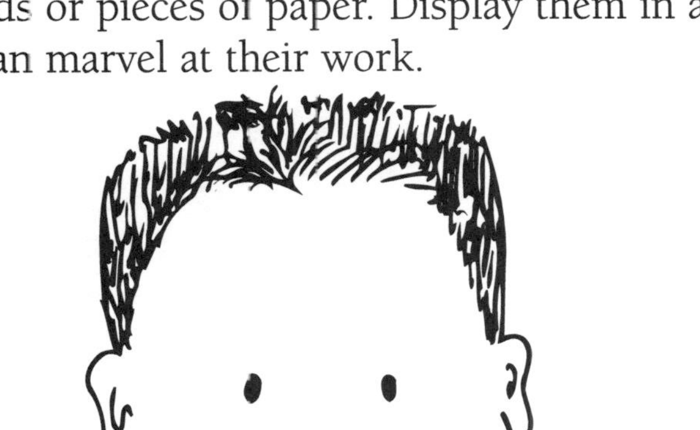

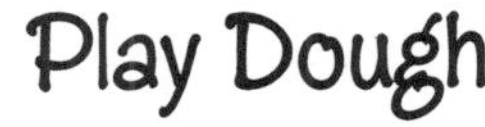

Play Dough

1 ½ cups water
2 tsp. liquid food coloring
2 tsp. cooking oil
2 cups flour
½ cup salt
4 Tbsp. cream of tartar
1 Tbsp. flavoring for a sensory smell

Mix water, oil, and food coloring along with flavoring in a mixing bowl. Place flour, salt, and cream of tartar into a large saucepan. Cook over medium heat, adding the liquid mixture slowly and stirring constantly. Cook and stir for five minutes, until a ball of dough forms. Let cool. Store in a refrigerator when not in use.

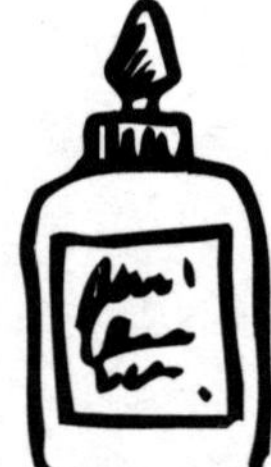

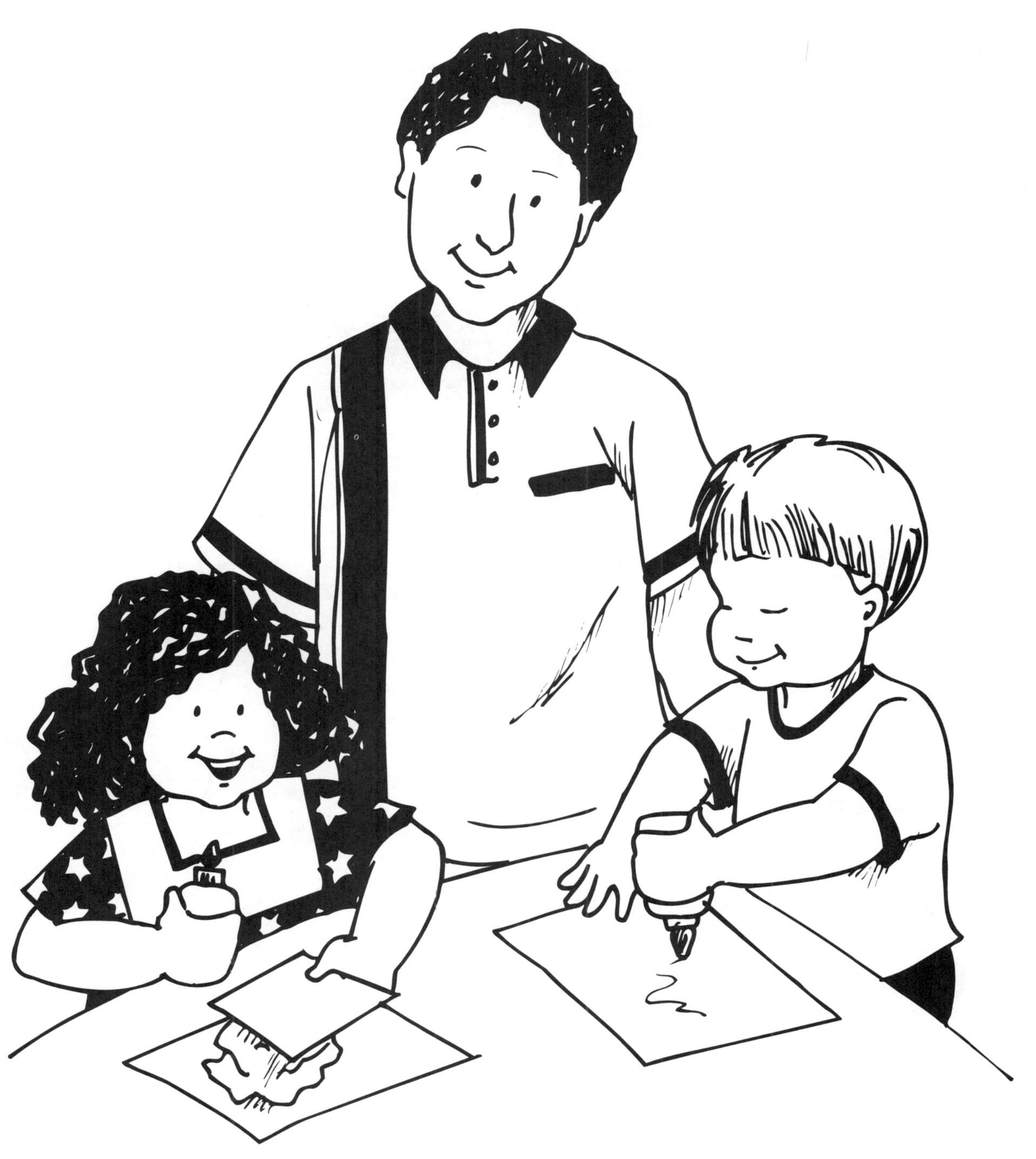

Gluing

Star Fun

Cut out a variety of different sizes and colors of stars for the children to use. Set out glue, glitter, tissue paper, aluminum foil, cotton, and the stars. Have the children glue the materials onto the stars. Next, encourage them to glue their stars all over a long sheet of paper. Or, you can hang them from the ceiling.

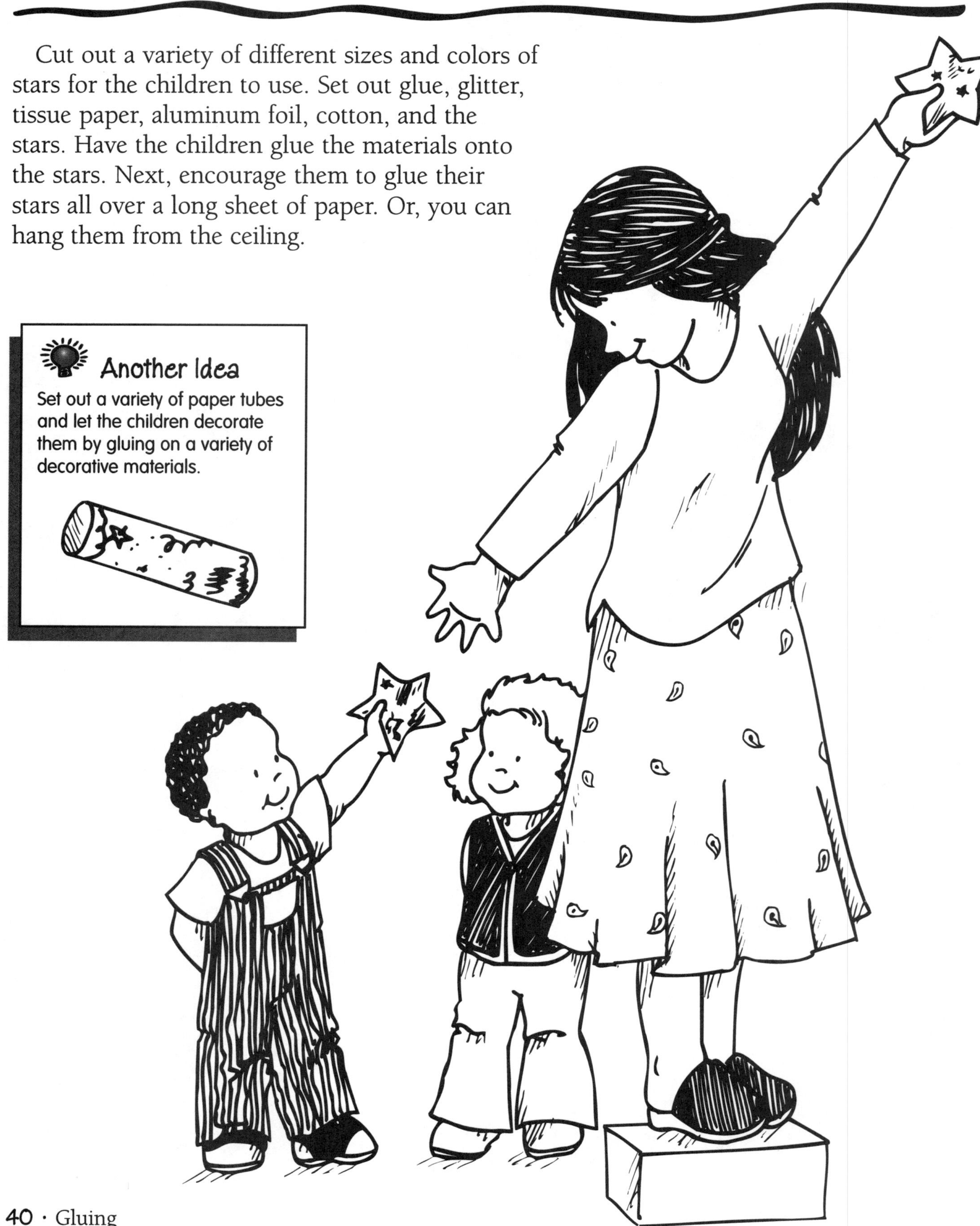

Another Idea

Set out a variety of paper tubes and let the children decorate them by gluing on a variety of decorative materials.

Super Streamers

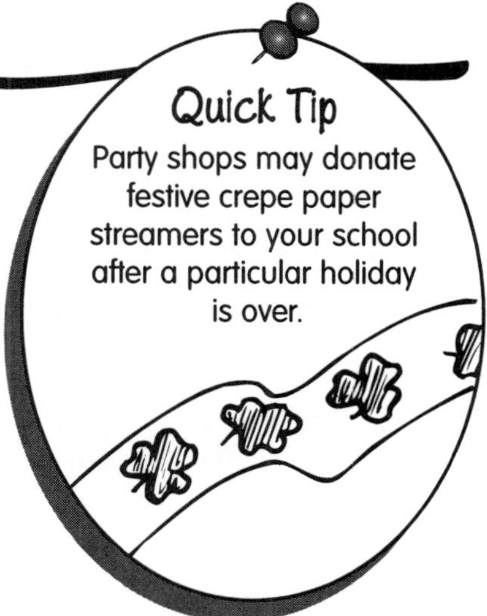

Have your children make colorful streamers to hang in the classroom. Set out a variety of different colored party streamers that you have cut into different lengths as well as glue and collage materials, such as feathers, stickers, paper shapes, metallic paper, ribbon, etc. Have the children glue collage materials onto their streamers however they wish. When the streamers are finished, let the children take them outside and run, holding their streamers. Then hang them in the classroom to create a colorful room.

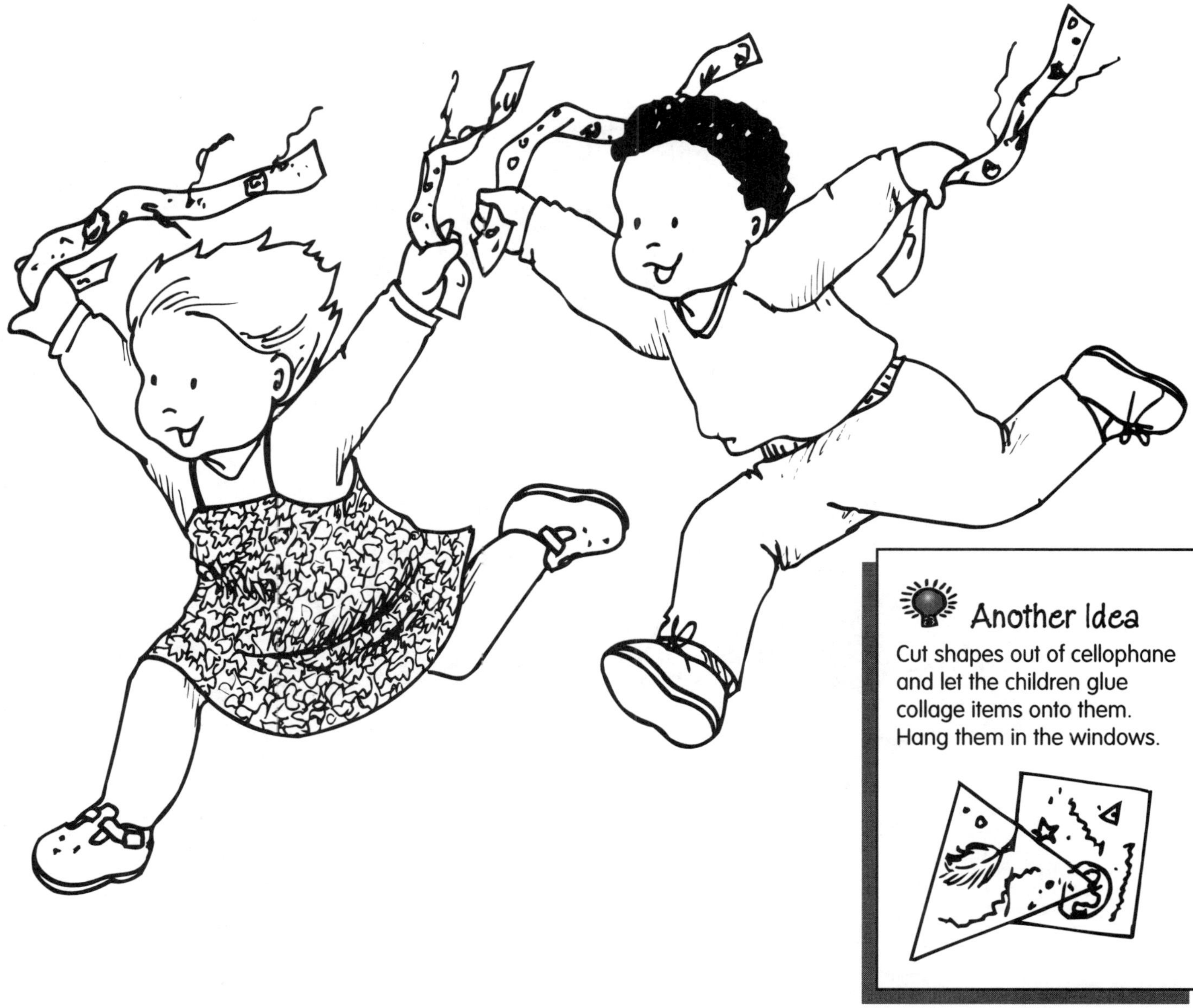

Another Idea

Cut shapes out of cellophane and let the children glue collage items onto them. Hang them in the windows.

Fantastic Wall Hangings

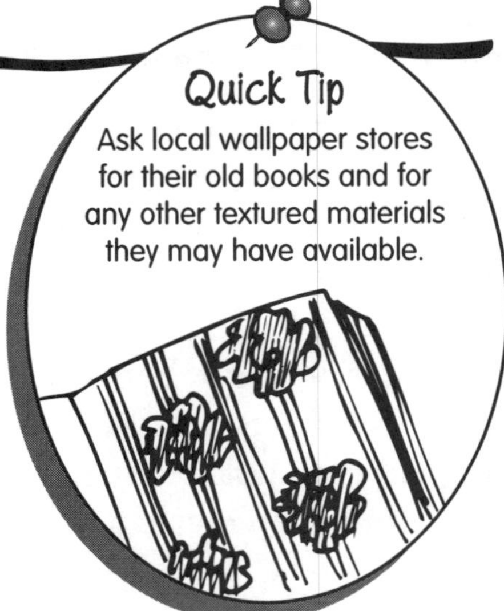

Cut burlap into rectangles, squares, and triangles. Be sure they are at least 10" x 10" so the children will have a good-size wall hanging.

Set out wallpaper, scissors, glue, and other materials like buttons, ribbon, etc., that the children can glue onto the burlap material. Encourage them to look through all the different types of wallpaper and cut it into different shapes and sizes before gluing.

When they have finished gluing, let their artwork dry. Hang their work up in the classroom when dry, or let the children take them home.

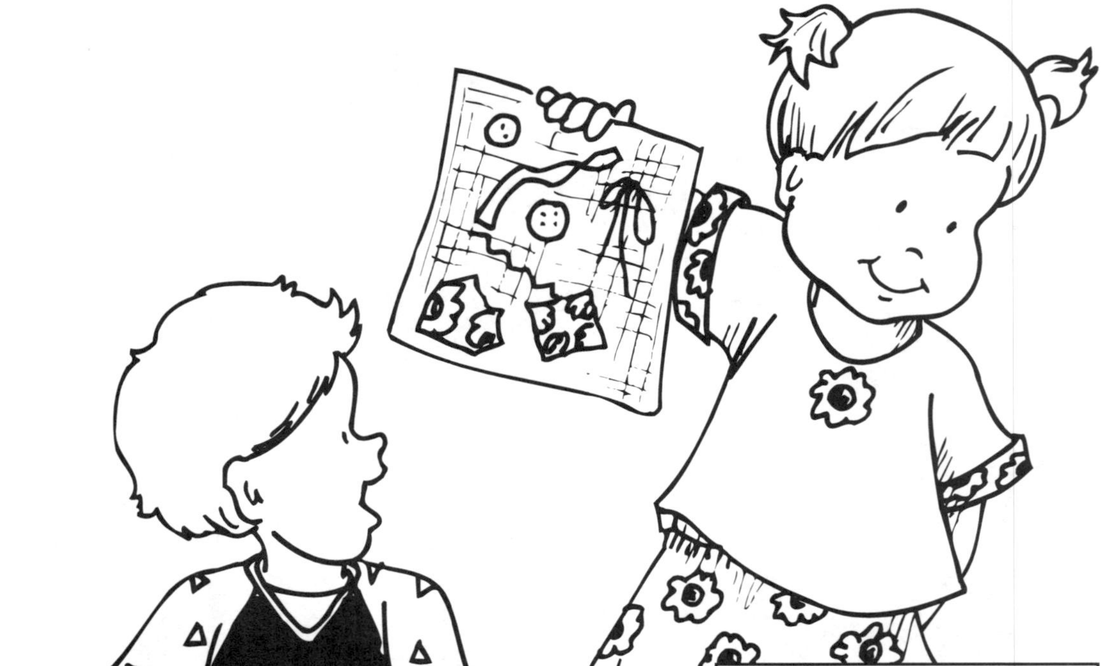

Another Idea

Let the children glue small tiles onto wood. These make bright wall hangings.

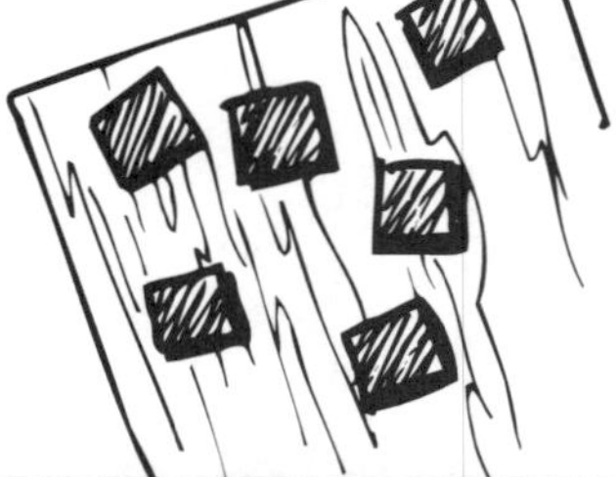

Texture Exploration

Set out paper and let the children use chalk to do brick, bark, sandpaper, or other textured rubbings. The children can compare the different textures produced from each object. Next, let the children glue their textures onto one large sheet of paper to produce a wall hanging that each child has contributed to. Have the children print their names on their textures. Hang the wall hanging with string or tape to be admired.

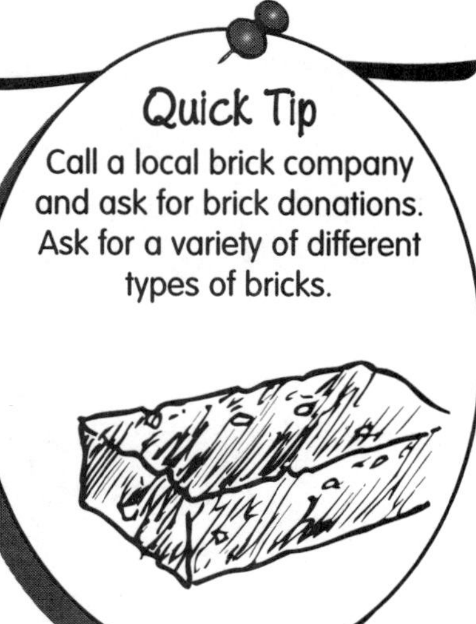

Quick Tip

Call a local brick company and ask for brick donations. Ask for a variety of different types of bricks.

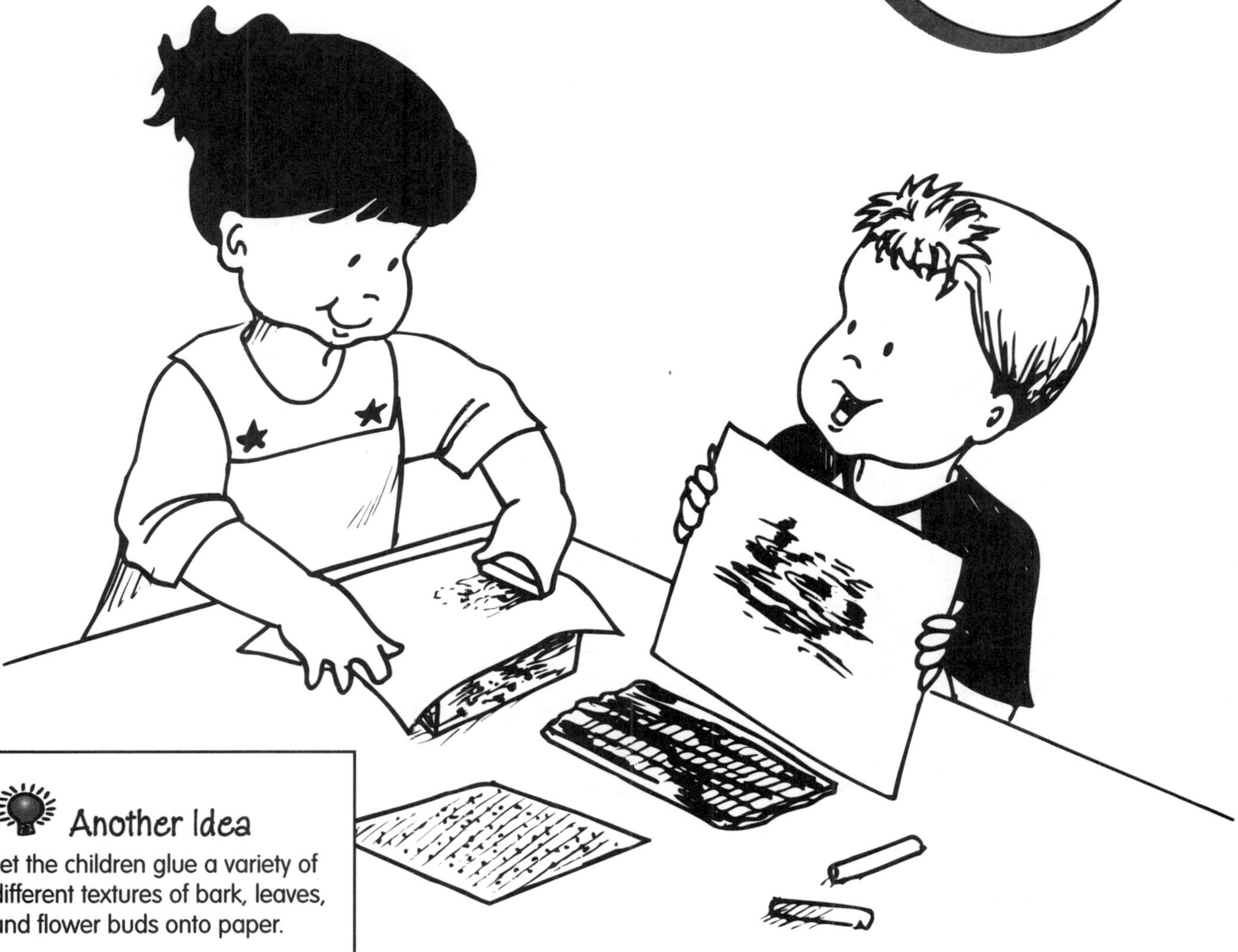

Another Idea

Let the children glue a variety of different textures of bark, leaves, and flower buds onto paper.

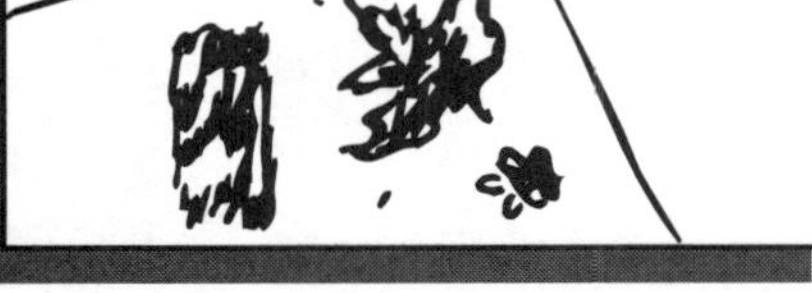

Colorful Shapes

Prepare a glue mixture by placing 3 tablespoons of glue in a small paint pot or plastic bowl. Add 1 tablespoon warm water. Mix well. Set out construction paper, tissue paper cut into shapes, paintbrushes, and the glue mixture.

Have the children sit down at a table and select a sheet of construction paper. Then have them select tissue paper shapes and put them on their construction paper. When they have completed this process, they are then ready to paint some glue mixture onto the shapes, creating various textures and changes in color.

When the children are done with the activity, have them place their work in an area to dry. Decorate the door entrance with their work.

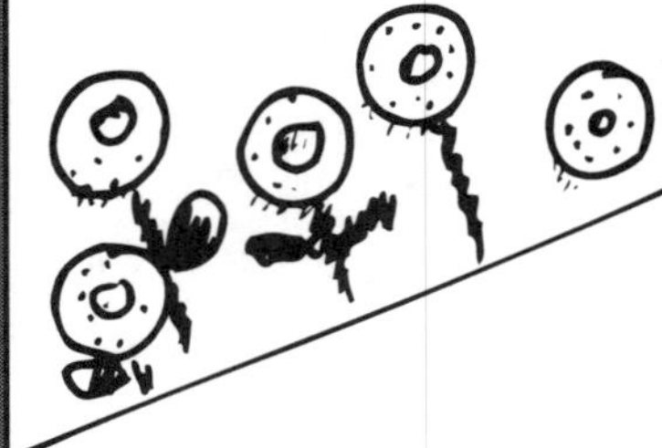

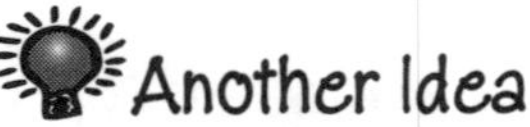

Another Idea

The children can create colorful pictures using glue, crayons, paper, and cereal. Let the children draw pictures and then glue colored cereal onto them.

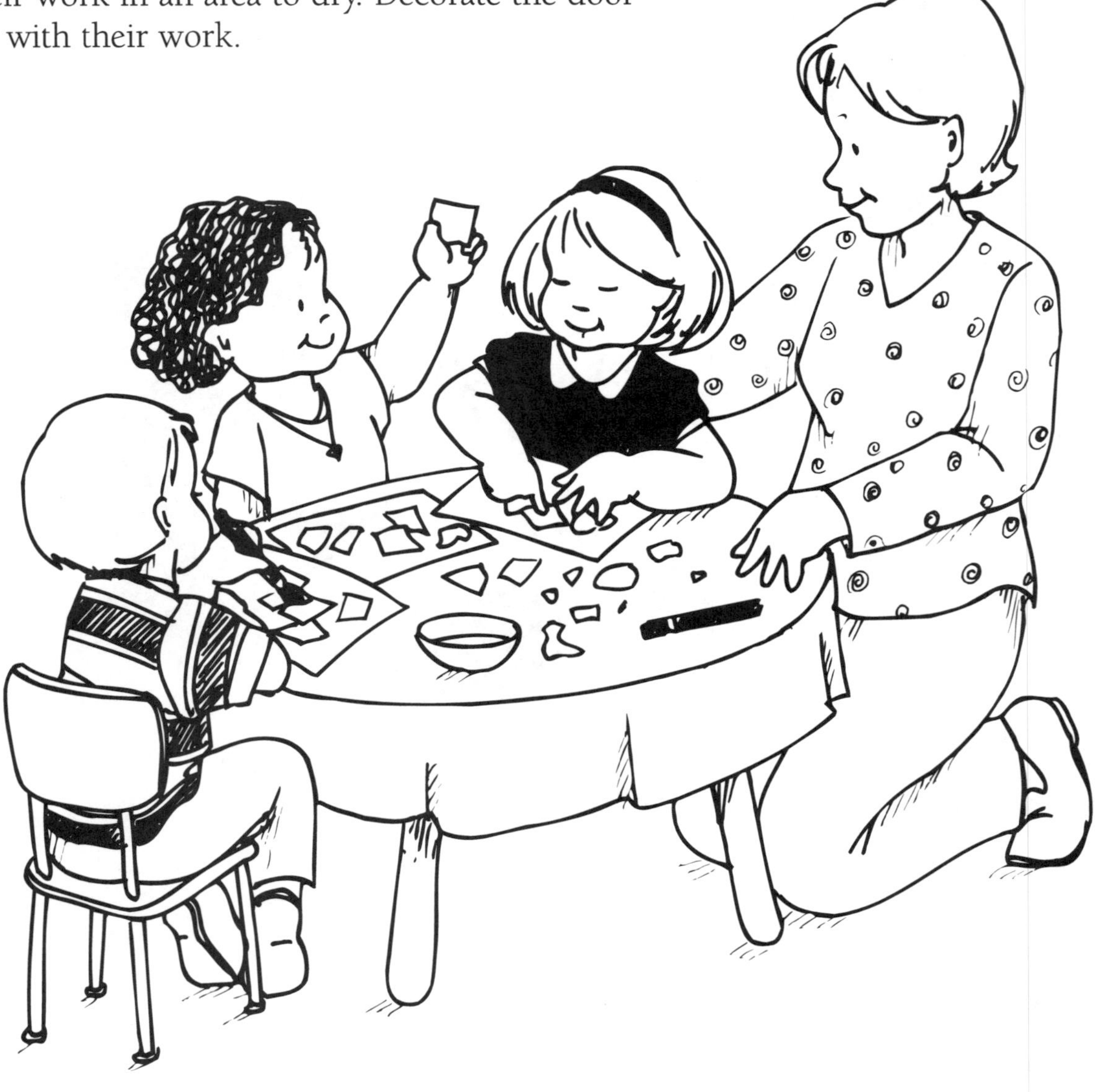

Picture This

Set out white and colored index cards along with glue, paper, scissors, magazines, and markers. Have the children create pictures on the cards using pictures cut from magazines and markers. Let them glue all of their cards onto a large piece of paper.

Quick Tip

Check with your local library to see if it has any old index catalog cards it can donate to your school.

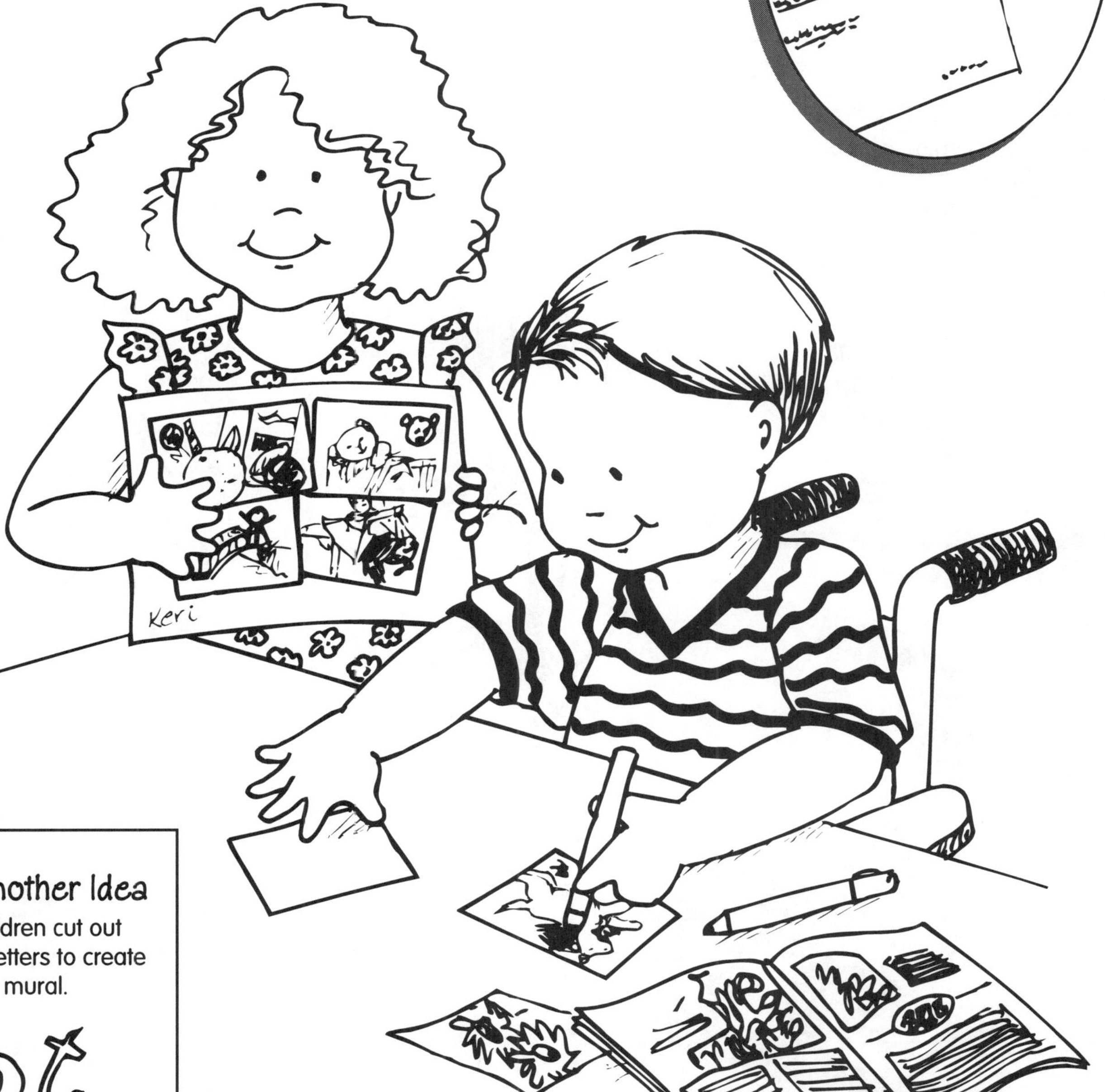

Another Idea

Let the children cut out words or letters to create a letter art mural.

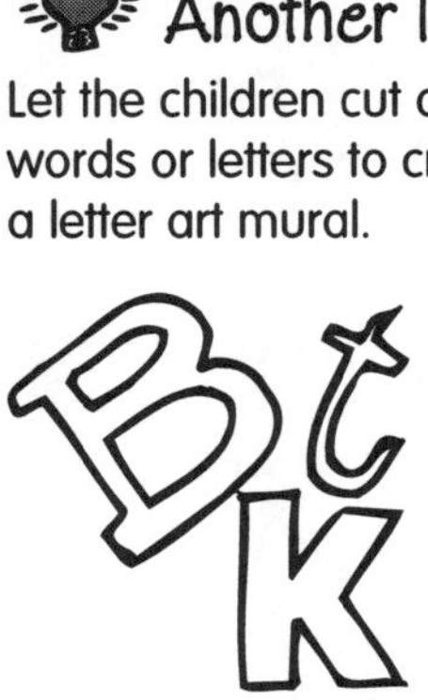

Flag Fun

Set out lightweight paper such as colored tissue paper or cellophane paper. Cut colored yarn and ribbon into strips. Have the children glue the decorative materials onto a piece of posterboard turned horizontally to create a class flag. You could also let the children create team flags. Hang the flags in the classroom with the creators' names attached.

Quick Tip

When the flags are dry, let the children discuss their flags at circle time.

Another Idea

Let the children make fabric flags by gluing pieces of fabric together on cookie sheets. Remove the glued fabric from the cookie sheet when dry.

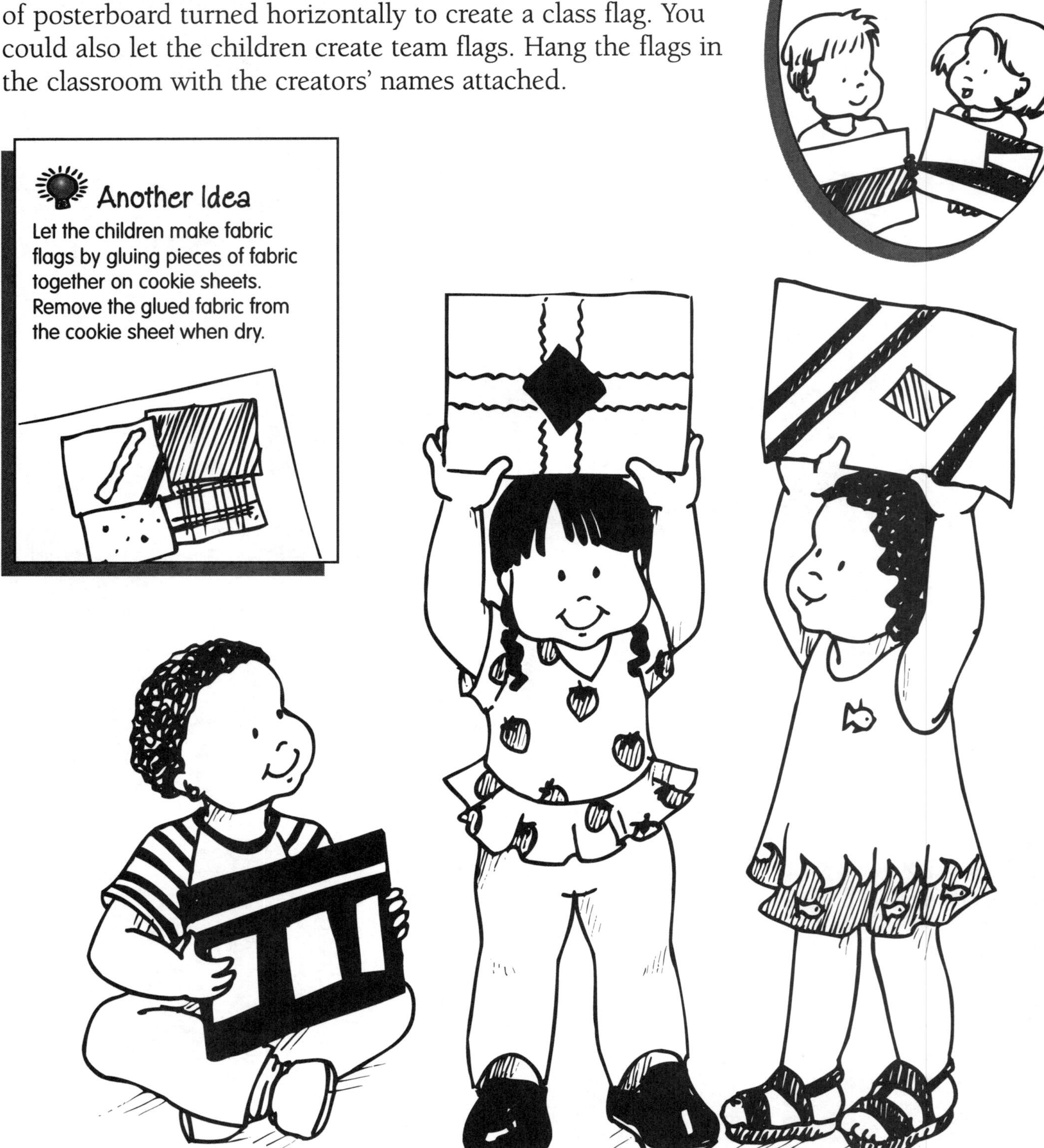

Dandy Decoupage

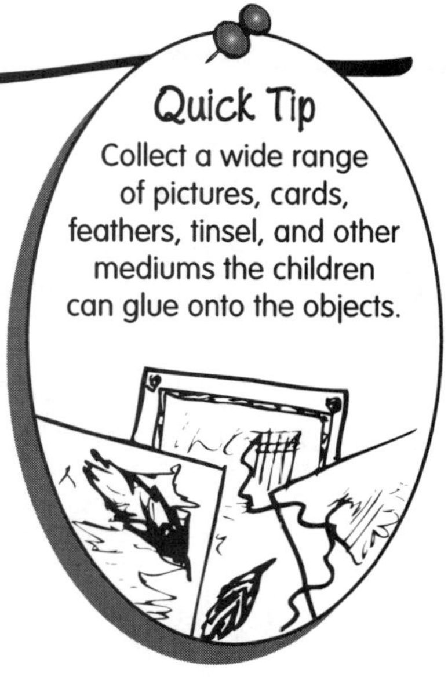

Prepare a decoupage mix using 4 tablespoons of glue to 1 tablespoon of warm water. Mix well.

Set out the decoupage mix, paintbrushes, and various objects that the children can glue pictures onto such as shoeboxes, paper towel tubes, clay pots, paper plates, paper, etc. Also set out scissors, magazines, and glue. Let the children find pictures in the magazines and cut them out. When they have finished cutting out a variety of pictures, show them how to glue the pictures onto the objects they have chosen. For example, if they selected a shoebox, show them how to put glue on the back of a picture and then glue it onto the box.

When they have finished gluing all their pictures, let them paint their pictures with the decoupage mix. Set aside and let dry. Display the children's finished objects on an art shelf. Write their names and the names of their projects on folded index cards and display these next to the objects.

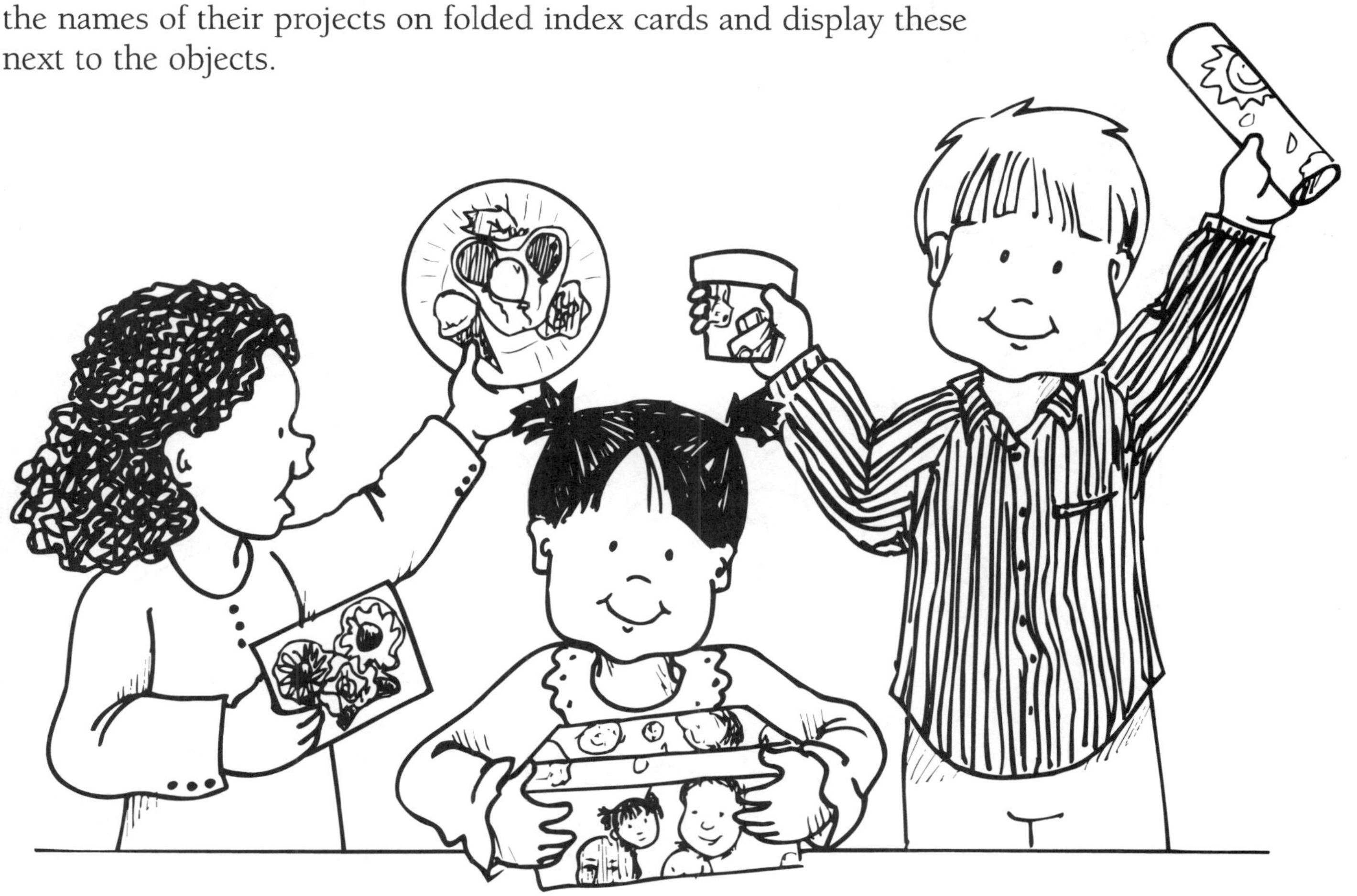

Paper and Cardboard Construction

Provide each child with a large piece of cardboard, scrap pieces of cardboard, a variety of different kinds of paper, glue, and scissors. Encourage the children to glue the scrap cardboard and an assortment of paper onto their large pieces of cardboard. Show them how to crinkle, stack, and glue the paper to provide a range of different textures. Let them glue pictures and create frames around the outside edges.

Quick Tip

College art teachers usually have a variety of scrap cardboard that they will donate to schools.

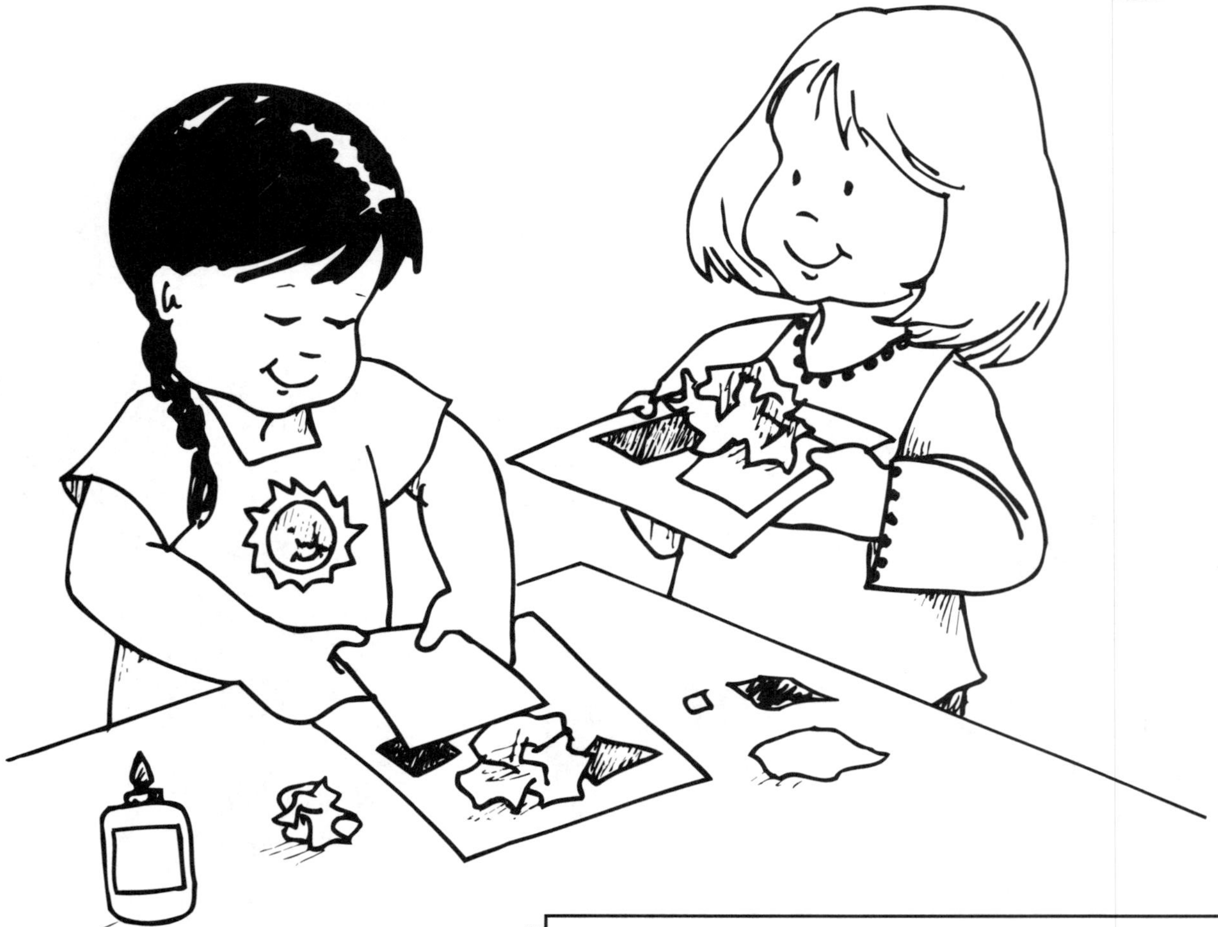

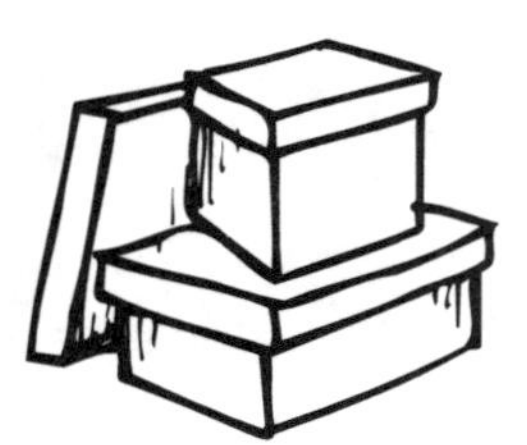

Another Idea

Provide the children with a variety of small cardboard boxes. Let the children glue the boxes together. They can glue paper onto their box creations for decorations.

Naturally Nice Nature Scenes

Ask parents and teachers to add to your nature collection. Have the children help you sort the nature items into art bins. Set out glue and paper of different sizes and textures on the art table. Set out the nature collection. Encourage the children to create nature scenes by gluing on various nature objects. Let them tell you all about their designs and creations. Be sure they print their names on their papers. Hang their work up on a clothesline outside so parents and others can enjoy!

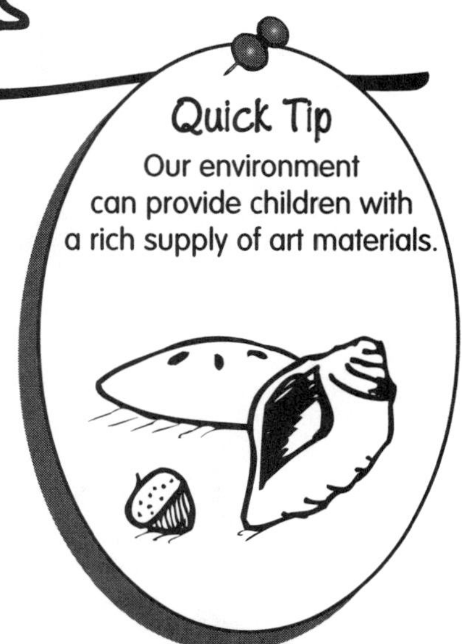

Quick Tip

Our environment can provide children with a rich supply of art materials.

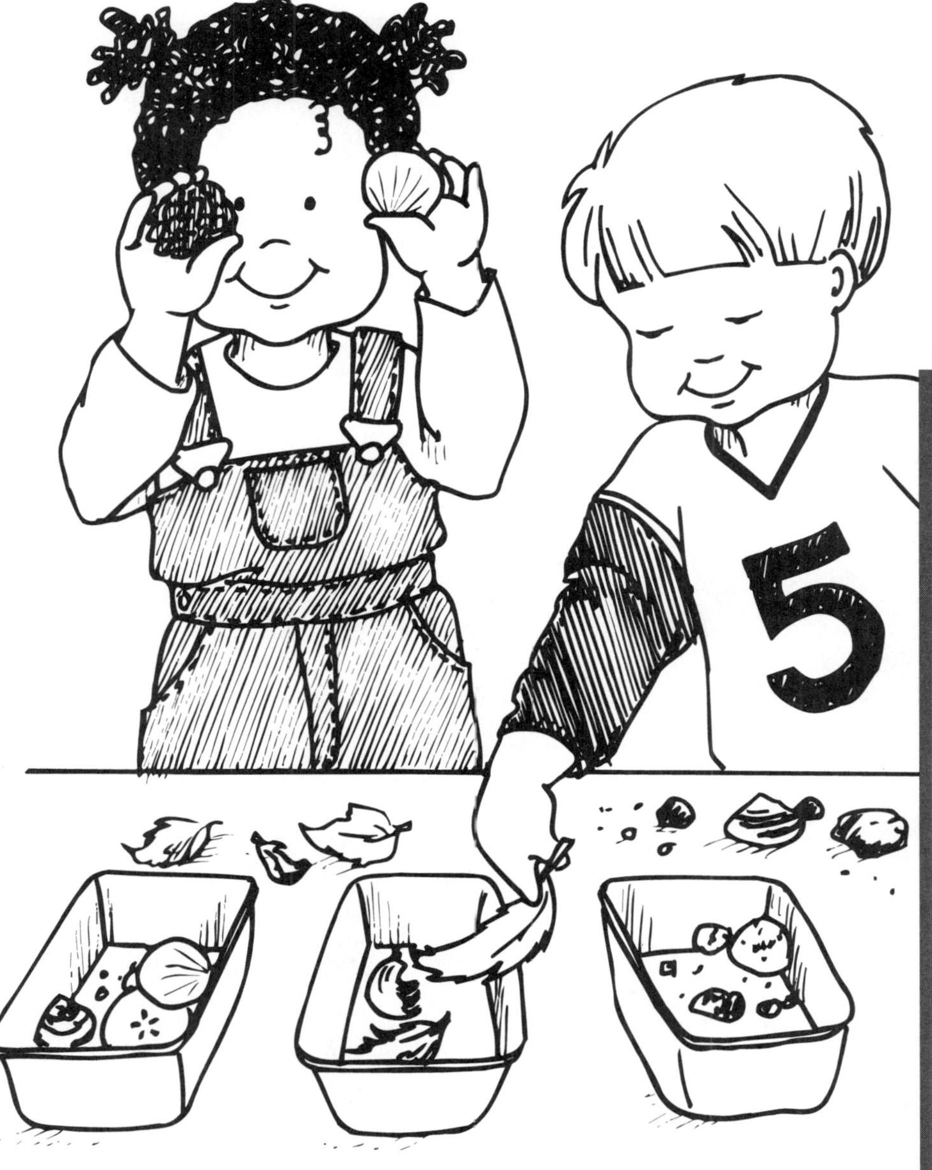

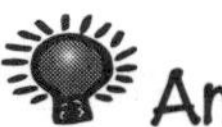

Another Idea

Set out bottles of glue and paper. Gather some sand and place it into plastic cups or bowls along with plastic spoons. Show the children how to squeeze the glue in long lines, shapes, patterns, or pictures on the paper. Show them how to sprinkle the sand onto the glue using the spoons. After all the glue is covered with the sand, help the children pick up the pictures and dump the remaining sand onto Styrofoam trays.

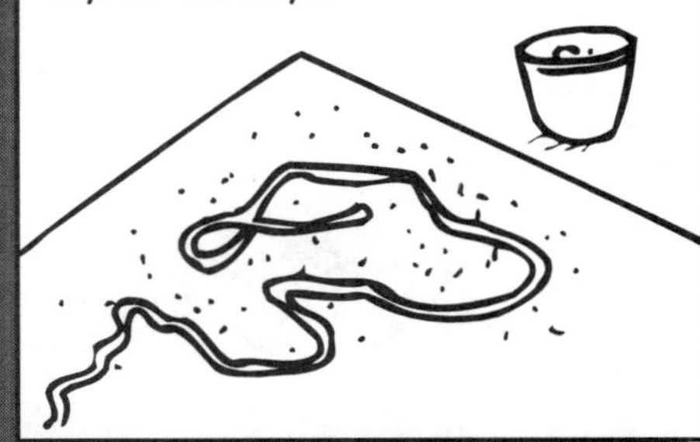

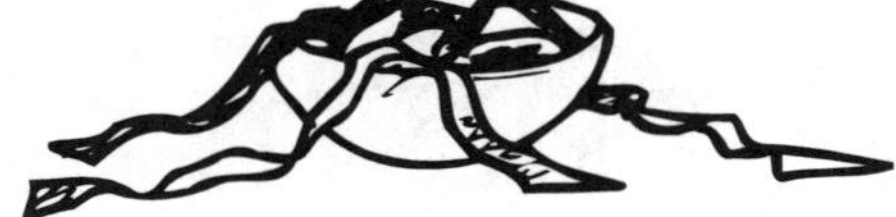

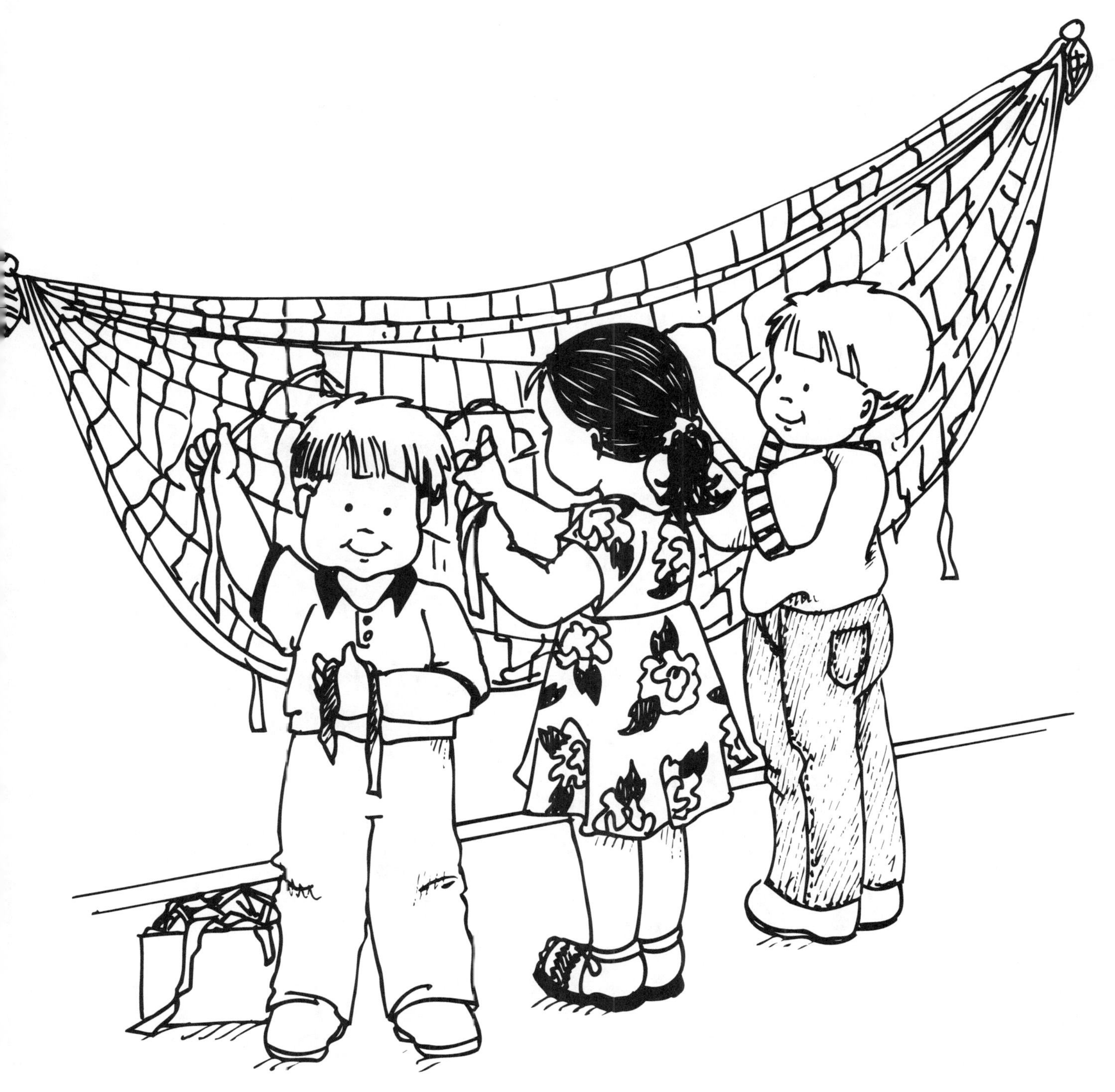

Weaving and Sewing

Card Creations

Provide the children with crayons, markers, construction paper, hole punches, and weaving and sewing materials they can use to create wonderfully textured cards. You can punch holes in the cards in random or planned order and the children can weave ribbon or yarn* through them. The children can then decorate the cards even more with crayons or markers. Let the children stretch their imaginations and make cards for special people.

*You will want to tape one end of each piece of yarn to aid in weaving.

Quick Tip

Go to a local fabric shop and ask if they will donate thread and other weaving materials that are going to be discarded.

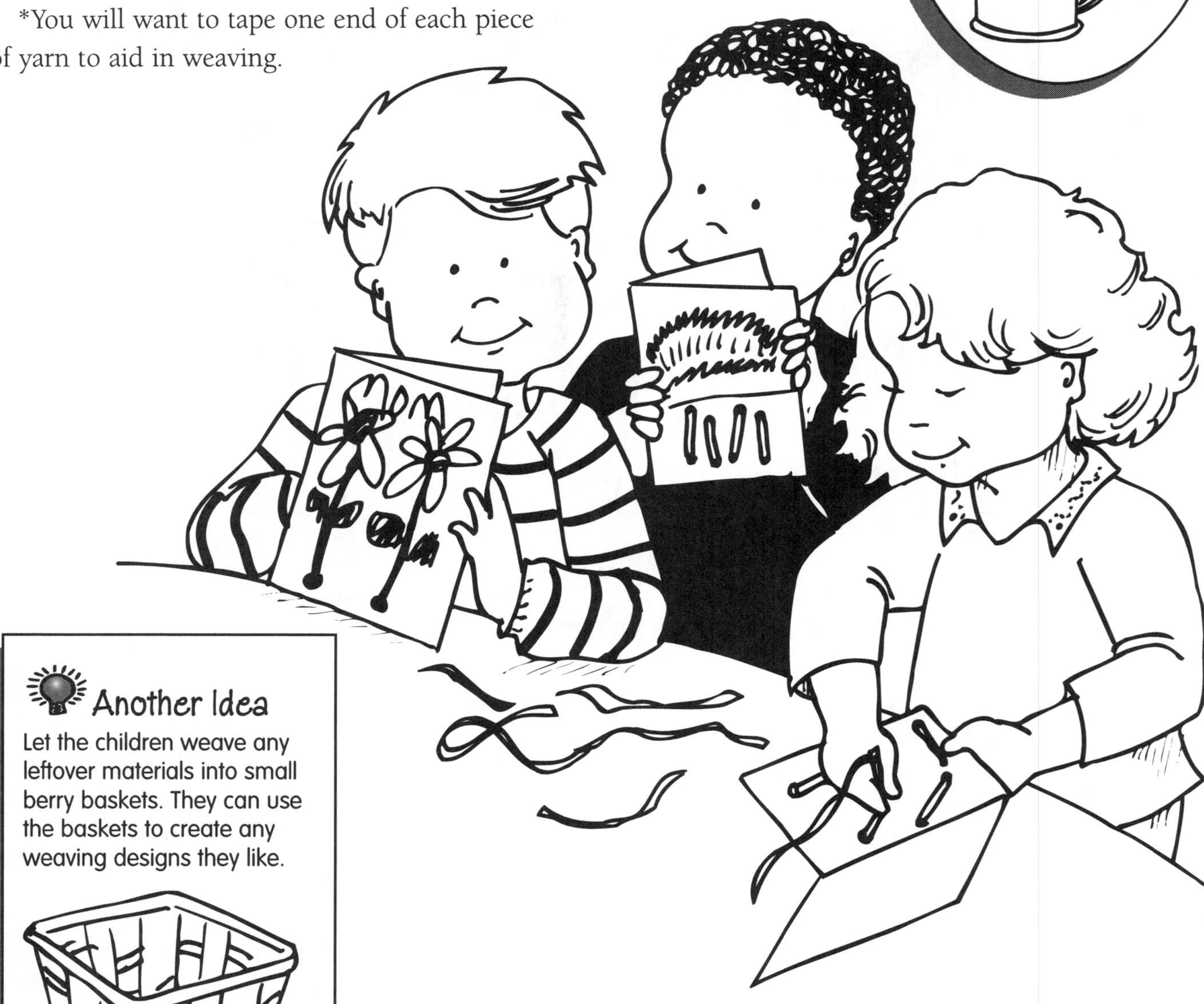

Another Idea

Let the children weave any leftover materials into small berry baskets. They can use the baskets to create any weaving designs they like.

Needle Know-How

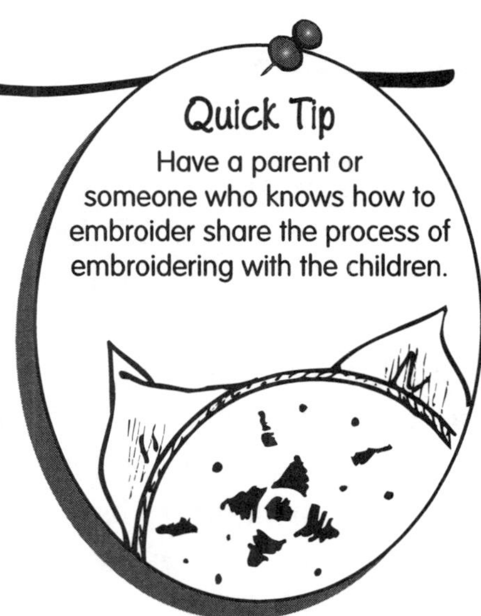

Quick Tip

Have a parent or someone who knows how to embroider share the process of embroidering with the children.

Borrow, purchase, and/or ask for donations of fabric scraps, embroidery thread, embroidery hoops, and dull pointed tapestry needles from parents or local craft stores. You will need at least five to seven hoops and needles. Place the material on the hoops and thread the needles with different colors of embroidery thread. Sit with the children and explain to them and demonstrate how to sew using an embroidery hoop. Let them explore and try to manipulate the thread, needle, and hoop. When they want to change colors, help them by threading the needles for them. After a child has finished, take the fabric off the hoop and let the child place the creation in a place to take home and share.

Another Idea

Provide the children with sewing cards made out of posterboard. You can cut them into flowers, butterflies, footballs, etc. Next, punch holes in them using a hole punch. Cut long strands of yarn, put tape on one end of each straw, and tape the other end of each to the posterboard. Let the children sew the shapes. Hang the shapes from the ceiling for an interesting look.

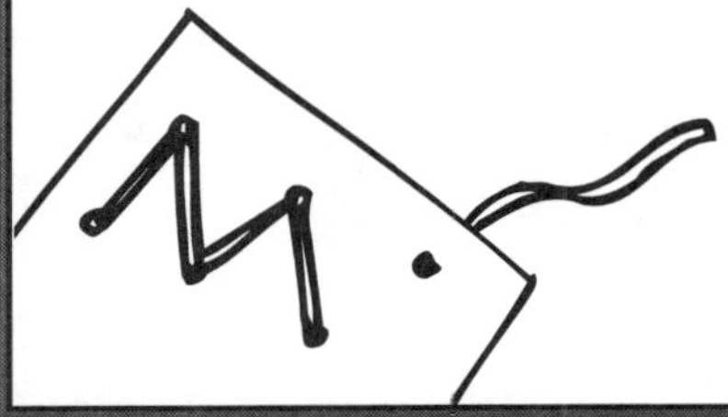

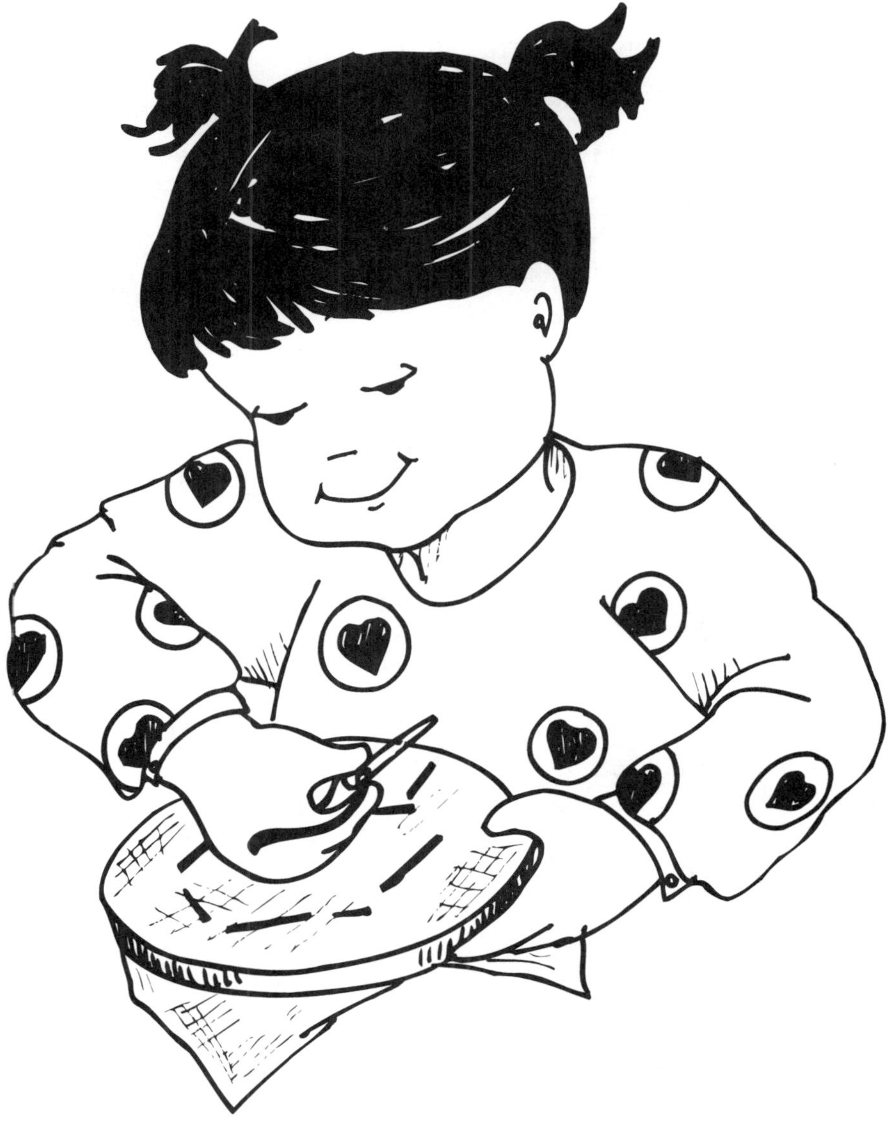

Under and Over

Gather old nets. Decide where to hang the nets, either inside or outside. If you choose to hang a net outside, the children can work on it each time you take them out. If you hang one inside, the children can add to it all week. Hang or tie the nets at the children's level. Cut out a variety of materials for the children to weave through the net, such as long fabric strips, holiday ribbon, long blades of grass, wild flowers with long stems, long feathers, etc. Encourage the children to bring in items from home to add to the class weaving project. Place the materials near the nets for the children to weave. The size of the nets will determine how many children can weave at one time. Hang up a piece of paper next to each net so that each child who has chosen to contribute to the creation can sign his or her name. Leave the class weavings up for a week or two.

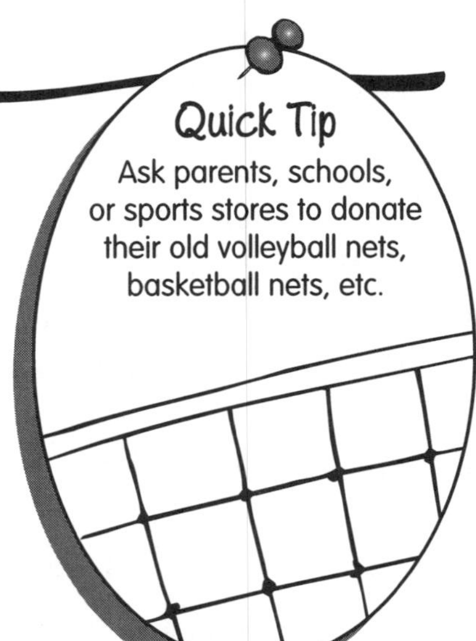

Quick Tip

Ask parents, schools, or sports stores to donate their old volleyball nets, basketball nets, etc.

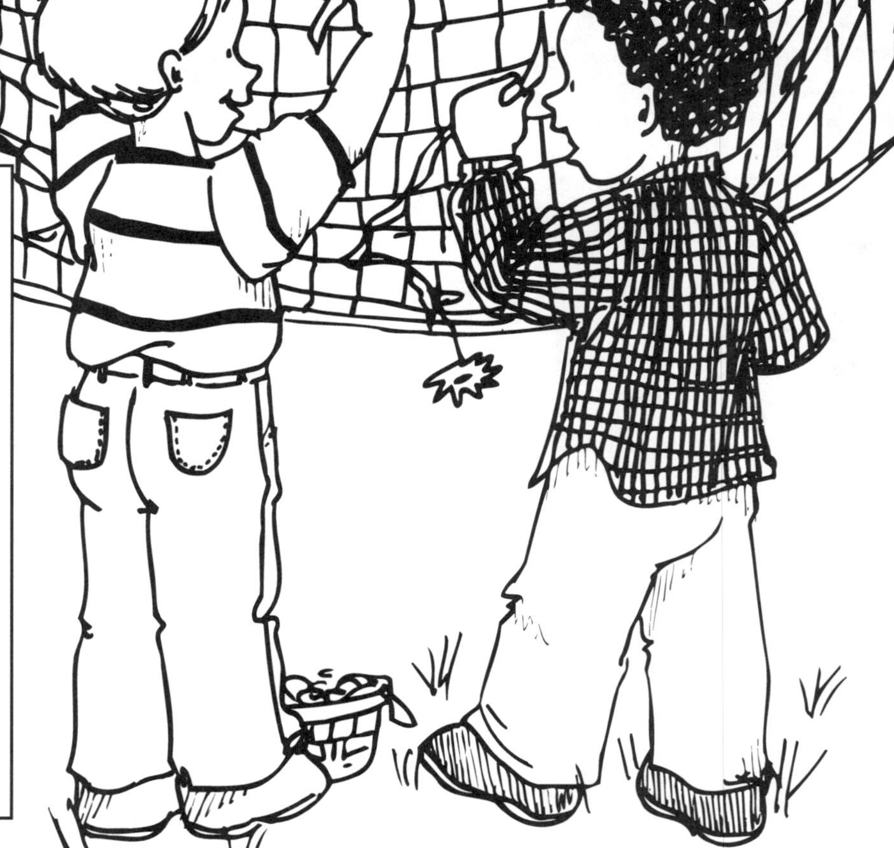

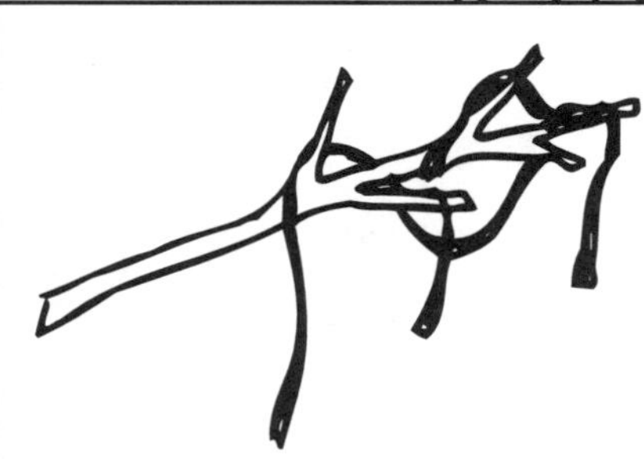

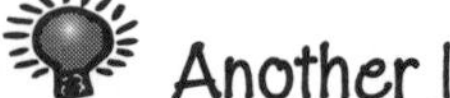

Another Idea

Gather tree branches (one per child) and set them in the art center. (The branches should be about one foot long and have at least four twigs that can be woven through.) Set out yarn, ribbon, tinsel, etc., the children can use to make their own special branch weavings.

Tiny Treasures

Collect small, durable boxes, about 5" x 5". Place four to five rubber bands across each box, spaced equally apart. Set the boxes out in the art center along with materials that the children can weave through the rubber bands such as yarn, ribbon, fabric, etc. Let the children have fun creating tiny treasure boxes. Display the boxes for the children to show to their parents and then let them take them home.

Quick Tip

Use small boxes such as gift boxes for jewelry.

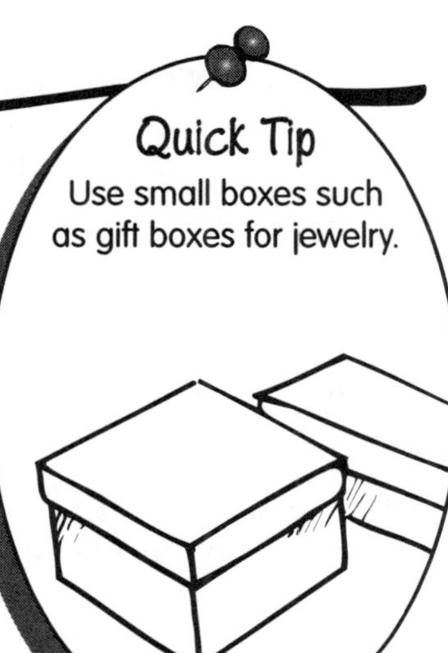

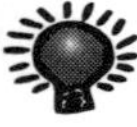

Another Idea

Purchase potholder makers that teach the children how to weave. These can be purchased at local discount stores. Set the weaving looms out with the first set of bands on them. Let the children take turns weaving on the looms at the art center. You will have to help the children finish the ends if they desire to complete the project. They will enjoy the process.

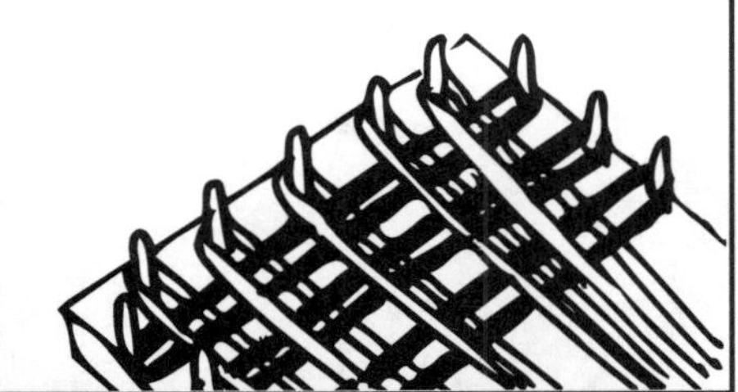

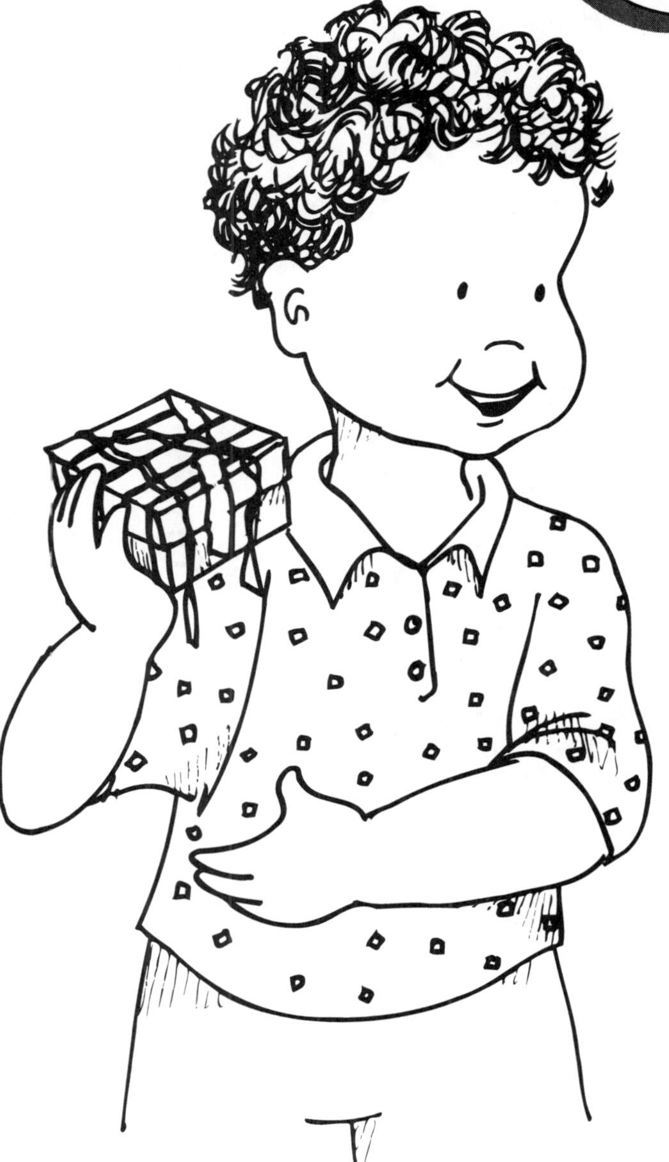

Thread Fun

Using pencils or paintbrushes, push holes through Styrofoam cups. Thread large plastic needles with yarn or embroidery thread, and encourage the children to sew, using different colors, through the cup holes. Then provide them with ribbon and other materials they can weave into their creations. At circle time, let the children talk about their creations. Set their creations out on a table and let them take them home at the end of the day.

Quick Tip

Girls' fine motor muscles develop faster than boys. Boys may need larger holes cut and more practice. This activity is a good prerequisite to printing.

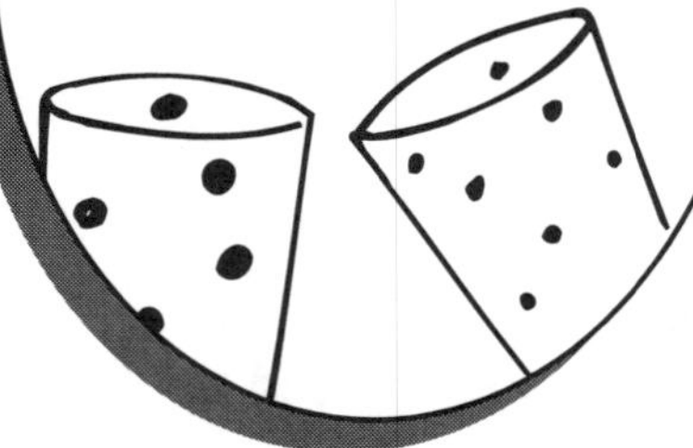

Another Idea

Use pencils to punch holes in foam trays. Set out ribbon, yarn, pipe cleaners, etc., the children can weave through the holes. Let the children take them home.

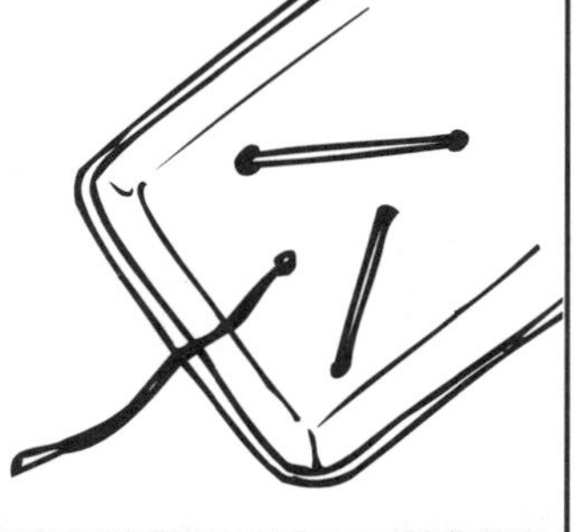

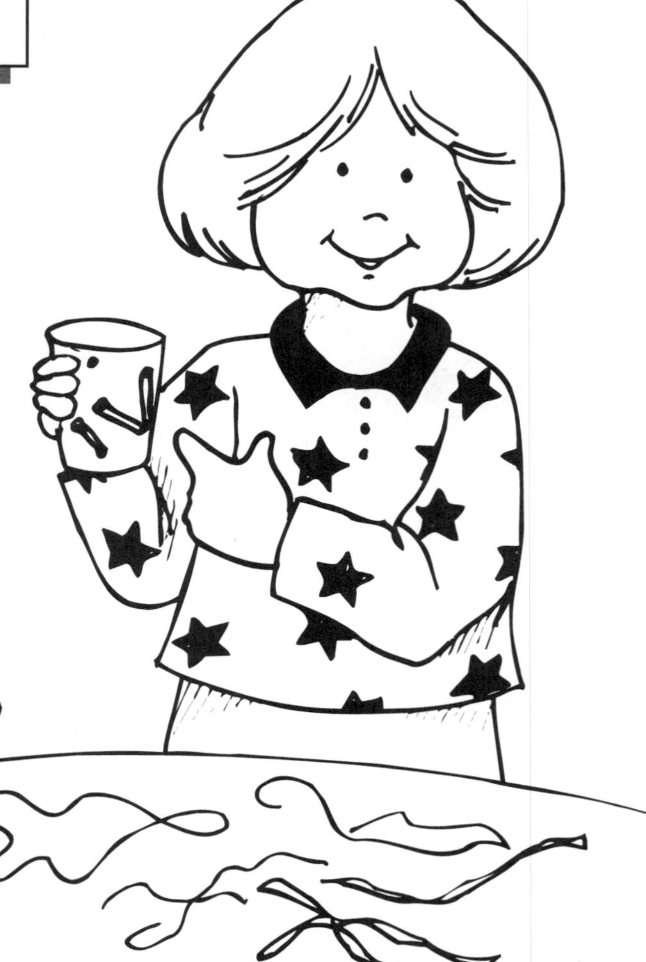

Look at Me!

Note: This is a good art project for open house.

Children can have a lot fun creating self-portraits by weaving yarn "hair" onto them. Punch at least 15 holes using a single hole punch in the top part of a paper plate for each child. Cut different lengths and colors of yarn and ribbon. Have the children look at themselves in small mirrors. Each child should then draw his or her face on a paper plate. Next, let the children select yarn or ribbon for "hair" and weave it through the holes in the plates. (To make it easier for the children, tape one end of each length of ribbon or yarn to the back of the plates so it is easy for the children to put it through a hole.) Hang the portraits on the children's chairs.

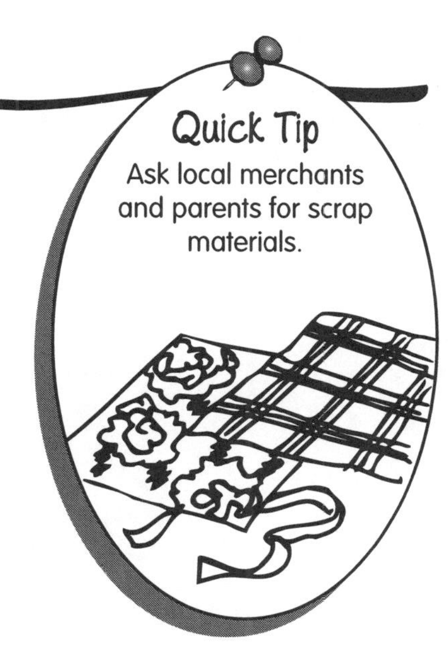

Quick Tip

Ask local merchants and parents for scrap materials.

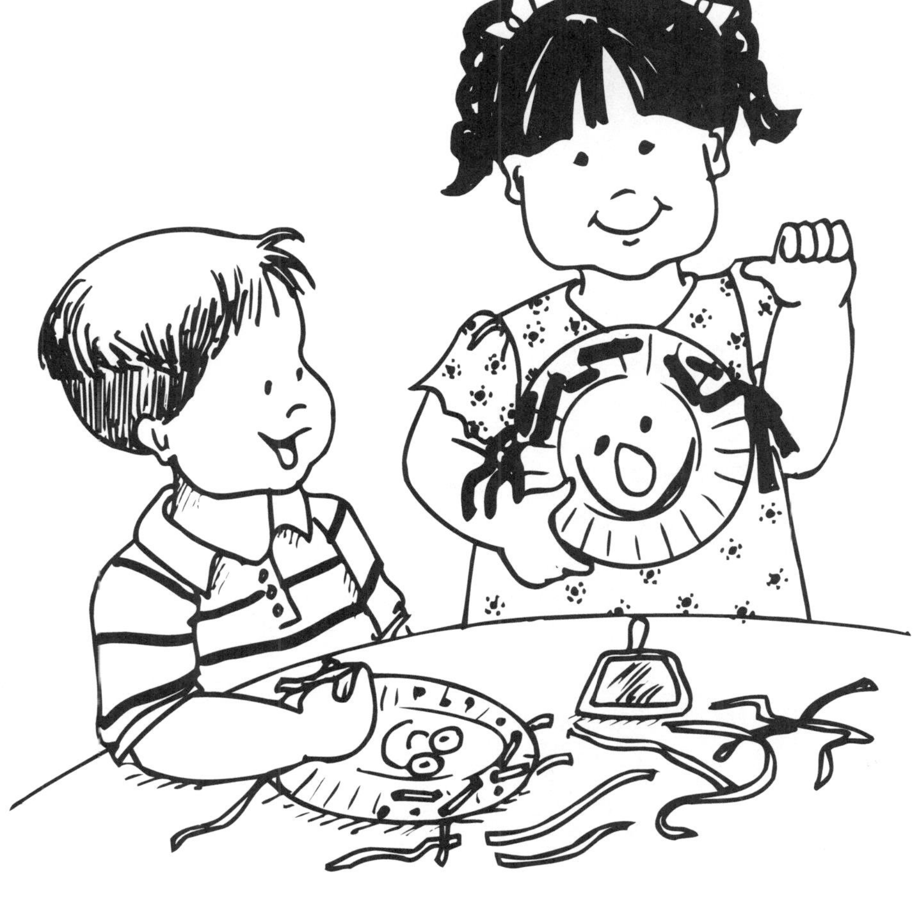

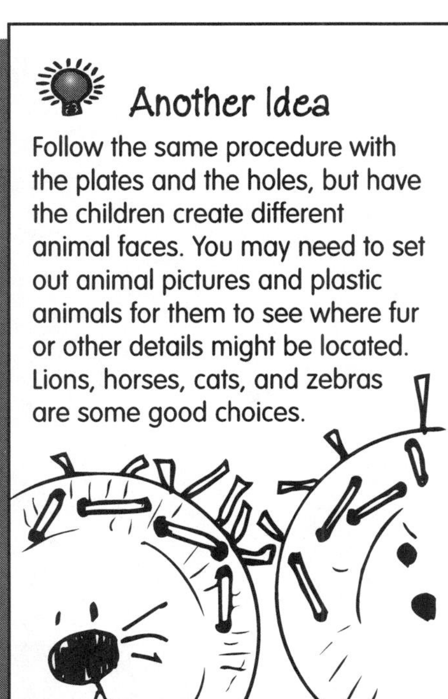

Another Idea

Follow the same procedure with the plates and the holes, but have the children create different animal faces. You may need to set out animal pictures and plastic animals for them to see where fur or other details might be located. Lions, horses, cats, and zebras are some good choices.

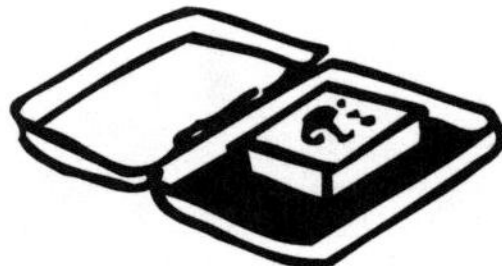

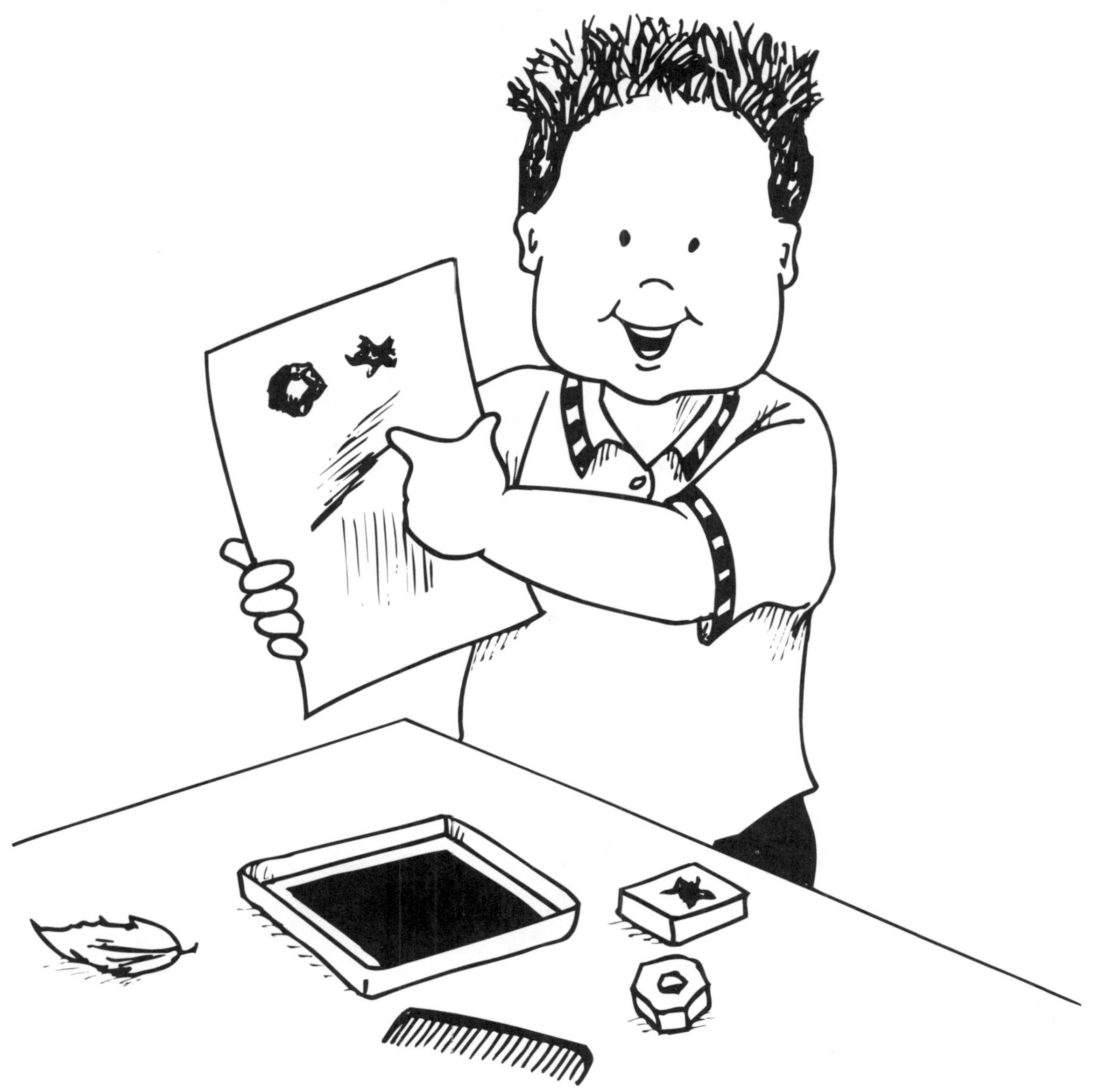

Printing

Gadget Fun

Another Idea

For Father's Day, let the children make cards using the gadgets. Send the cards home with some other special treats the children have made such as cookies, pottery, or a framed work of art.

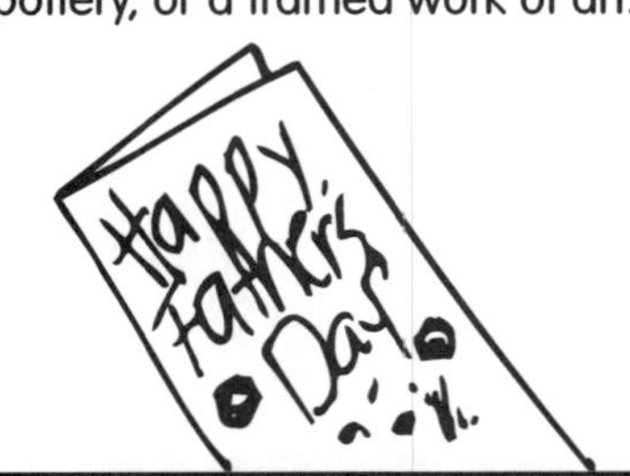

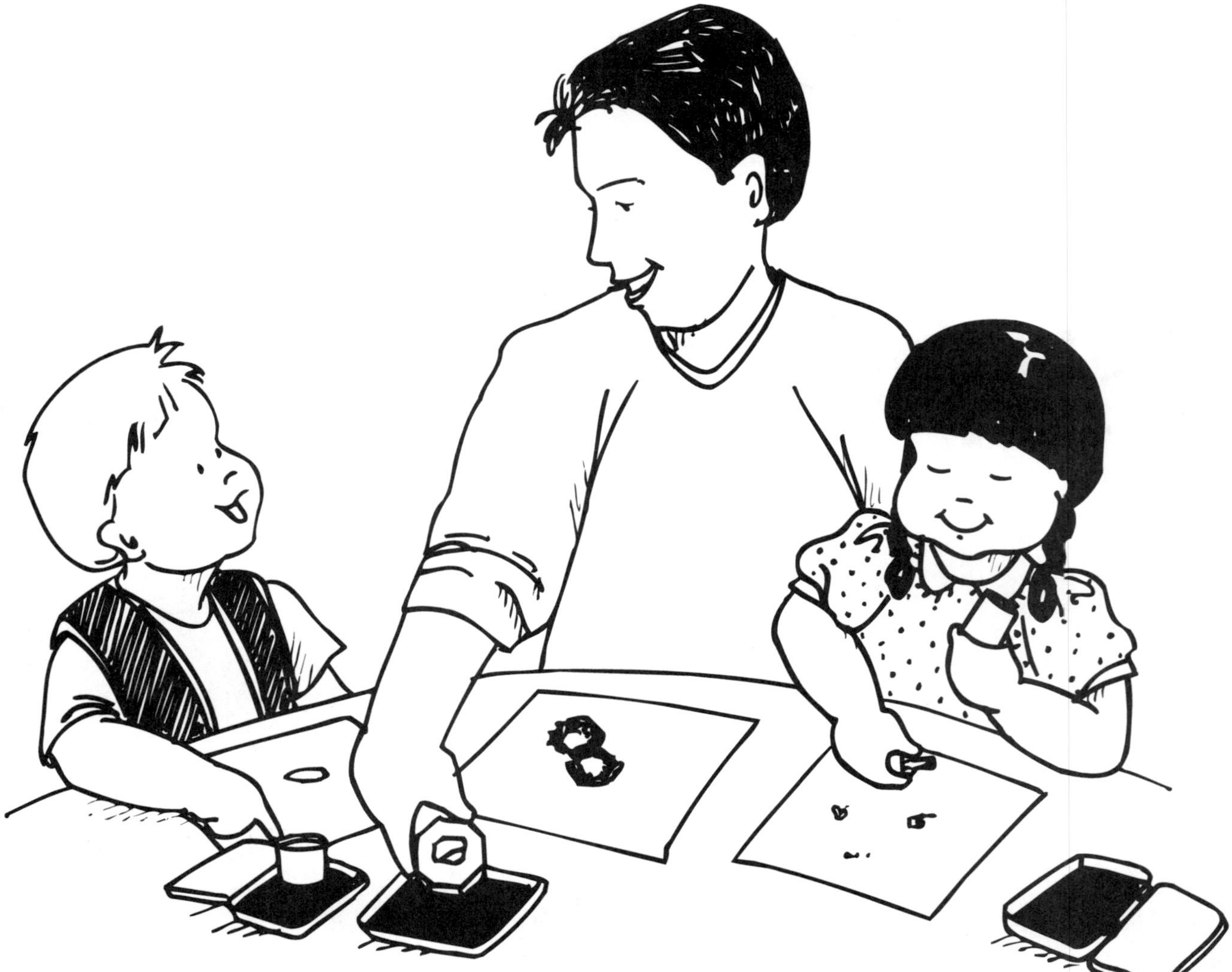

Gather a variety of different gadgets from parents, local building supply stores, or the maintenance department at your school. Ask for items such as PVC pipe (it comes in many different shapes and sizes), large nuts, bolts, wood scraps, and other items that the children can use for printing. Set the gadgets in the art center and tell the children the names of the different materials. Set out a variety of colored stamp pads and all sorts of paper cut into various shapes and sizes. Next, show the children how to put one end of a chosen gadget on an ink pad. Let them stamp the inked objects onto their papers to create prints. Encourage the children to tell you about their print creations and discuss their selection of gadgets.

Bow Prints

Ribbon bows come in many different shapes, sizes, colors, and textures. Set out a large variety of paper and bows and different colors of paint you have put on Styrofoam trays. Tell the children to dip the bows in the paint to create Bow Prints all over their papers. They can make placemats, cards, or just wonderful prints. After they dry, hang them on a clothesline for the children to look at throughout the week.

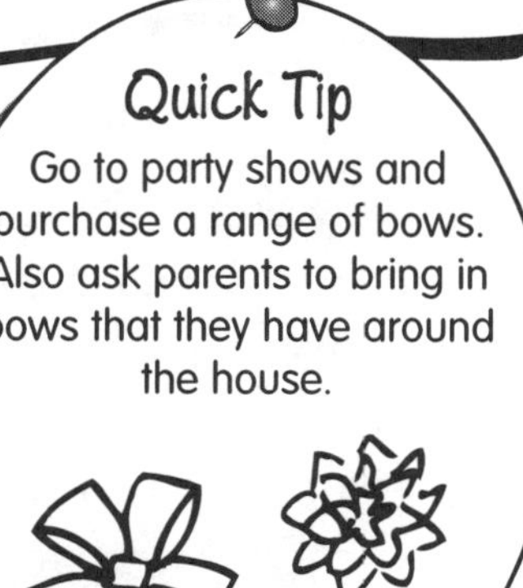

Quick Tip

Go to party shows and purchase a range of bows. Also ask parents to bring in bows that they have around the house.

Another Idea

Mix glitter in the paint and let the children try bow printing with glitter paint. To make glitter paint, mix 2 tablespoons paint with 1 teaspoon glitter.

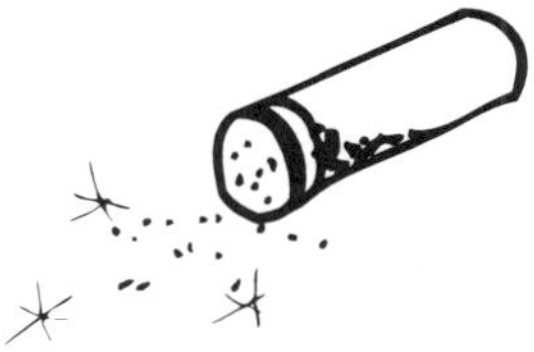

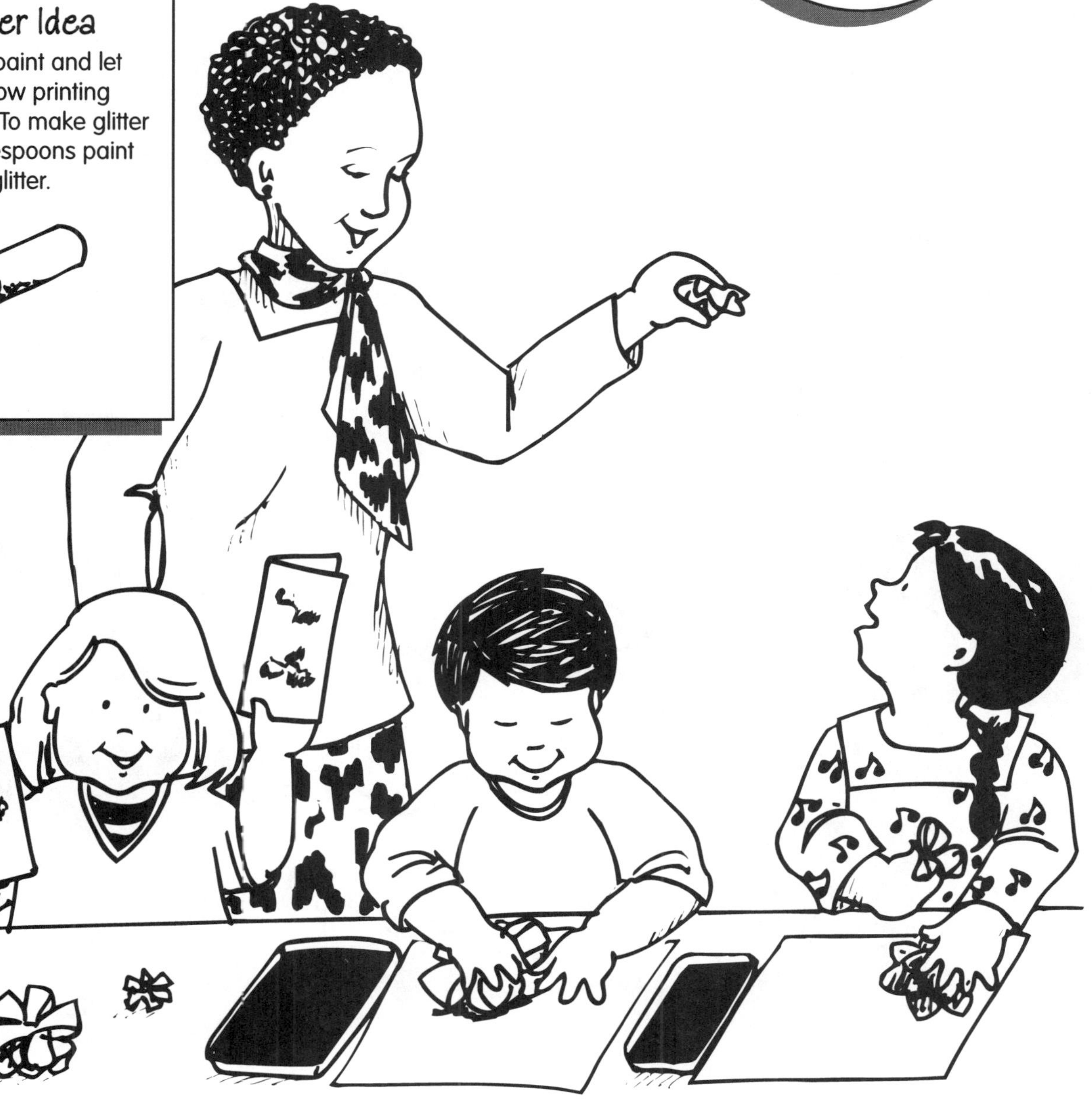

Bubble Prints

Mix 1 cup of Joy™ liquid dishwashing detergent to ¾ gallon of water. (You can mix the mixture in a plastic gallon jug, just be sure to leave enough room to be able to shake the mixture.) Next, add blue or green food coloring to the mixture. Pour the mixture into a large tub outside. Use a straw to make lots of bubbles. Then have the children take turns pressing white paper gently on top of the bubbles. (Make more bubbles when they start popping.) Set the papers out to dry and then hang them on a plastic shower curtain to create a mural.

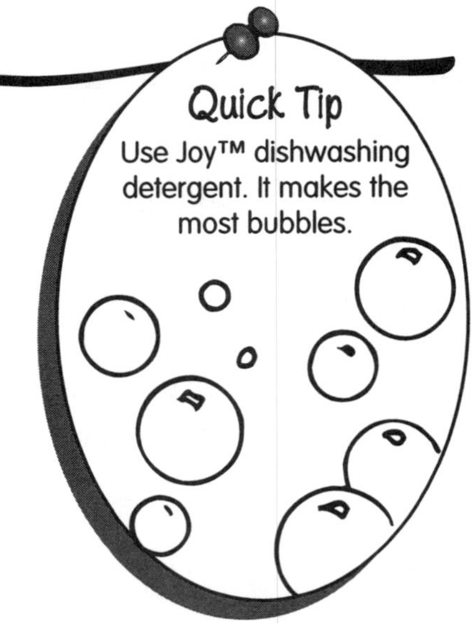

Another Idea

Hang white paper outside on a fence or set it on outside tables or sidewalks for the children. Then give the children misting bottles full of colored water they can use to make water prints. Let the children use several colors on their papers. They will create rainbow tie-dye prints.

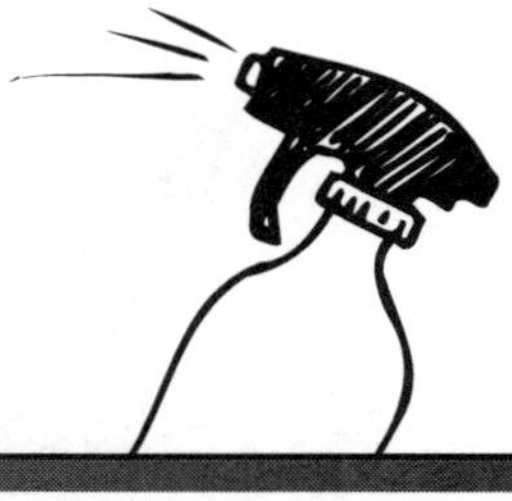

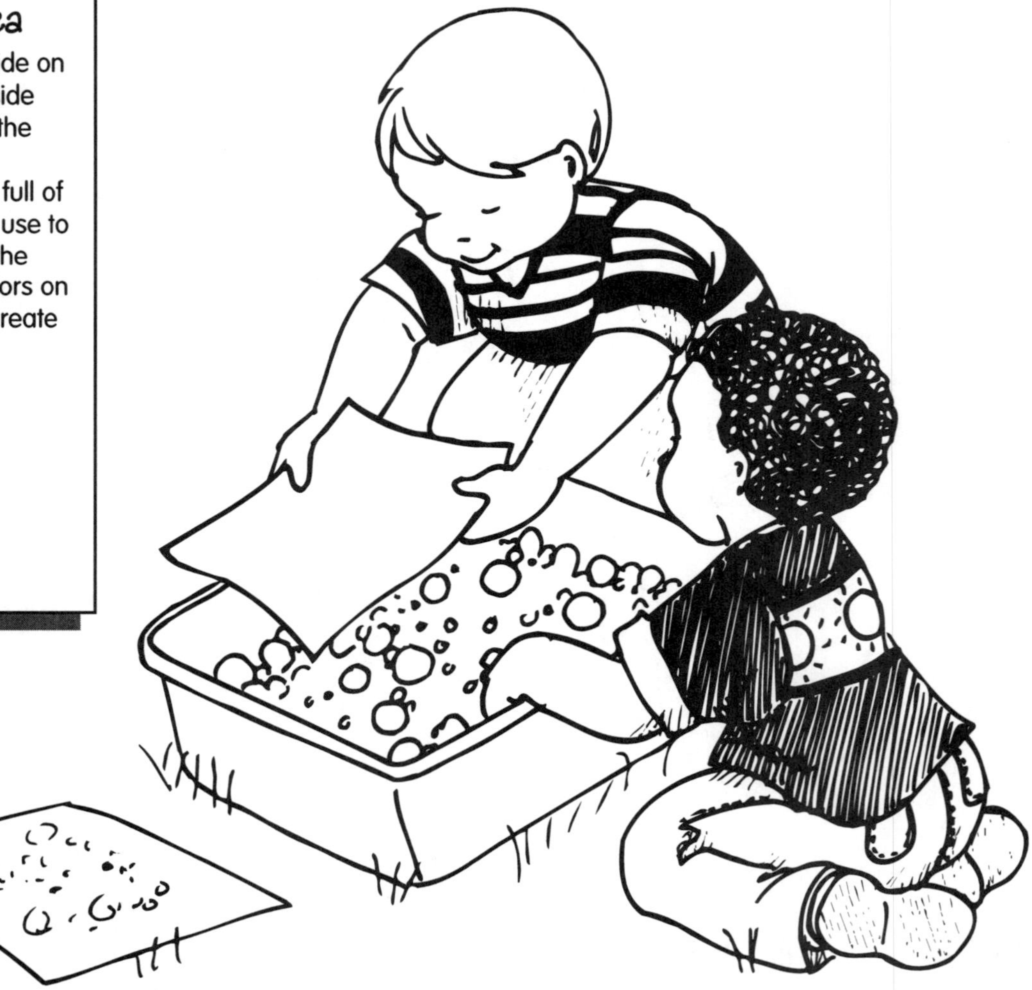

Kitchen Capers

Collect materials from your kitchen department, or ask parents to donate some. You can also find lots of used kitchen items at thrift shops. Here are just a few of the items you can use: potato mashers, dishwashing sponges (the kind with handles), cookie cutters, plastic scouring pads, plastic cups, etc.

Set out a variety of paper, the kitchen materials, and small plastic bowls filled with small amounts of paint. Put art smocks on the children. Show them how to dip the kitchen materials in the paint and then press the objects onto their papers. Let their artwork dry, and then send their creations home.

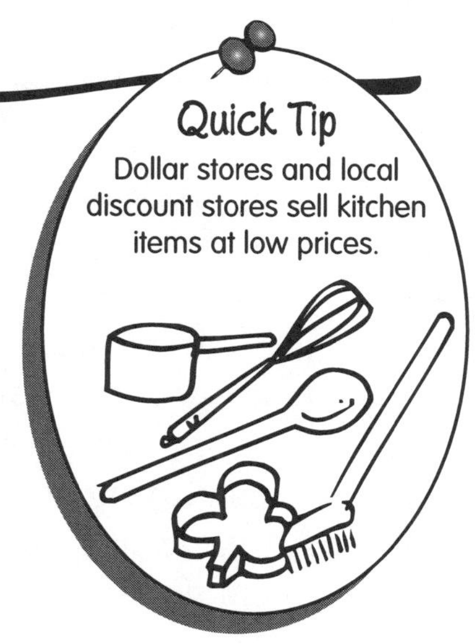

Another Idea

Using paper and paint in the same manner as stated above, give the children a variety of paper cups to use as circular print creations. Paper cups come in many different shapes and sizes. You can show the children how to do a large circle print and then put a smaller circle print inside a larger one.

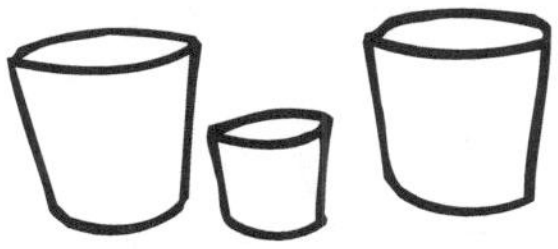

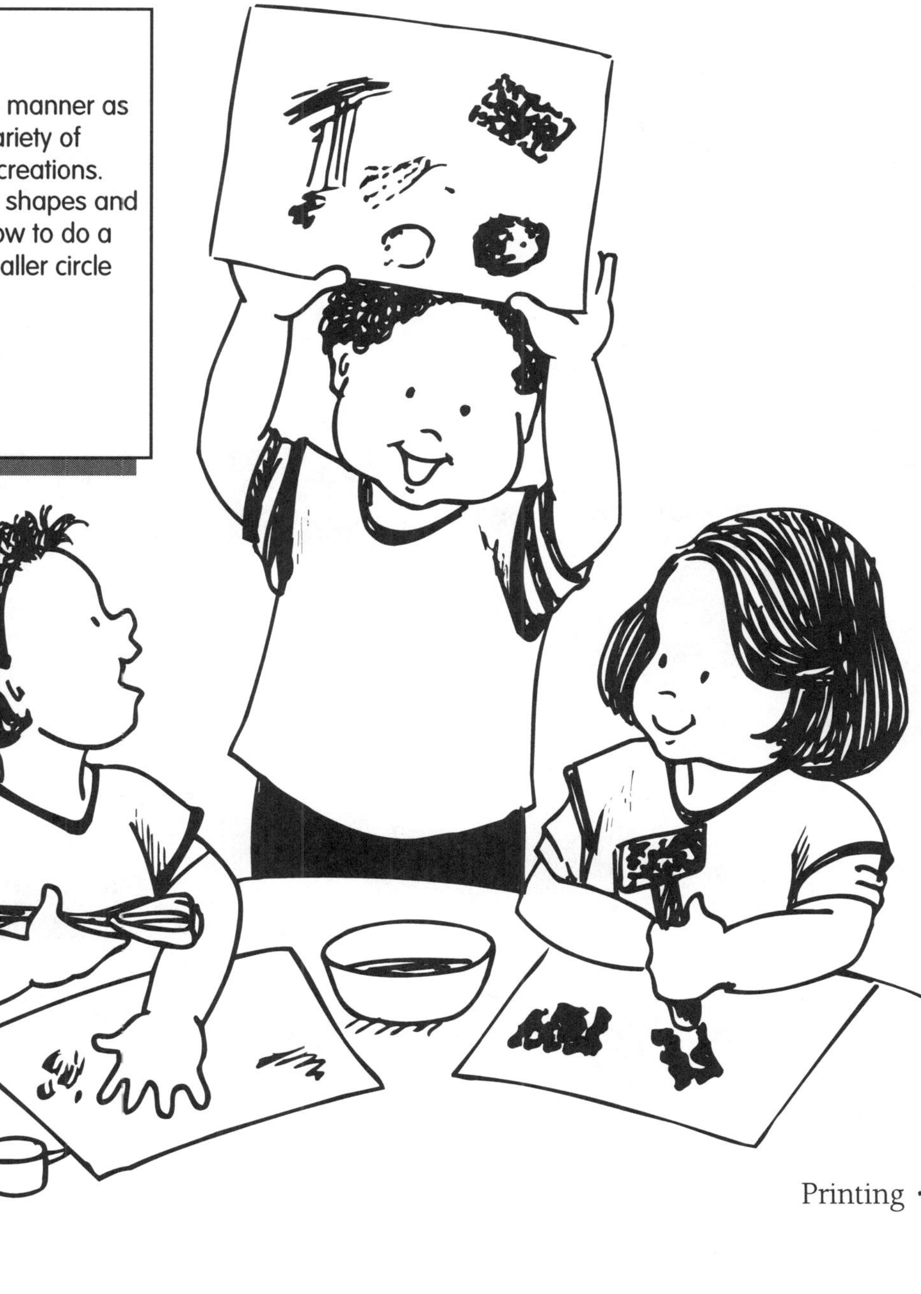

Twirls Swirl

Set out a variety of combs (large tooth, fine tooth, comb picks), different sizes of toothbrushes, and different types of brushes. Set out paper and small amounts of paint on foam trays. Have the children put on paint smocks. Have them use the tools to make prints by dipping the ends of the combs, brushes, and toothbrushes in the paint and then gently pressing the materials onto the paper, creating prints. You can also encourage the children to move the combs and brushes in a swirling motion to create different looks. Let them dry and hang them outside for the other children to marvel at.

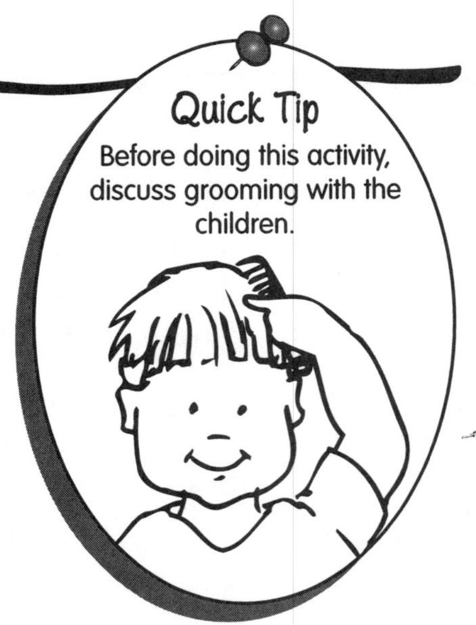

Quick Tip

Before doing this activity, discuss grooming with the children.

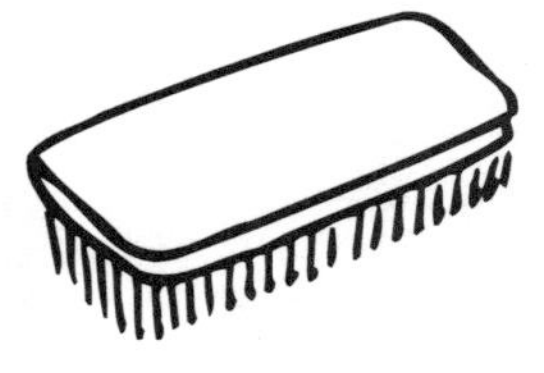

Another Idea

Use scrub brushes and water in buckets to do print art with water on sidewalks on a sunny day. You can also do this activity with paint and paper.

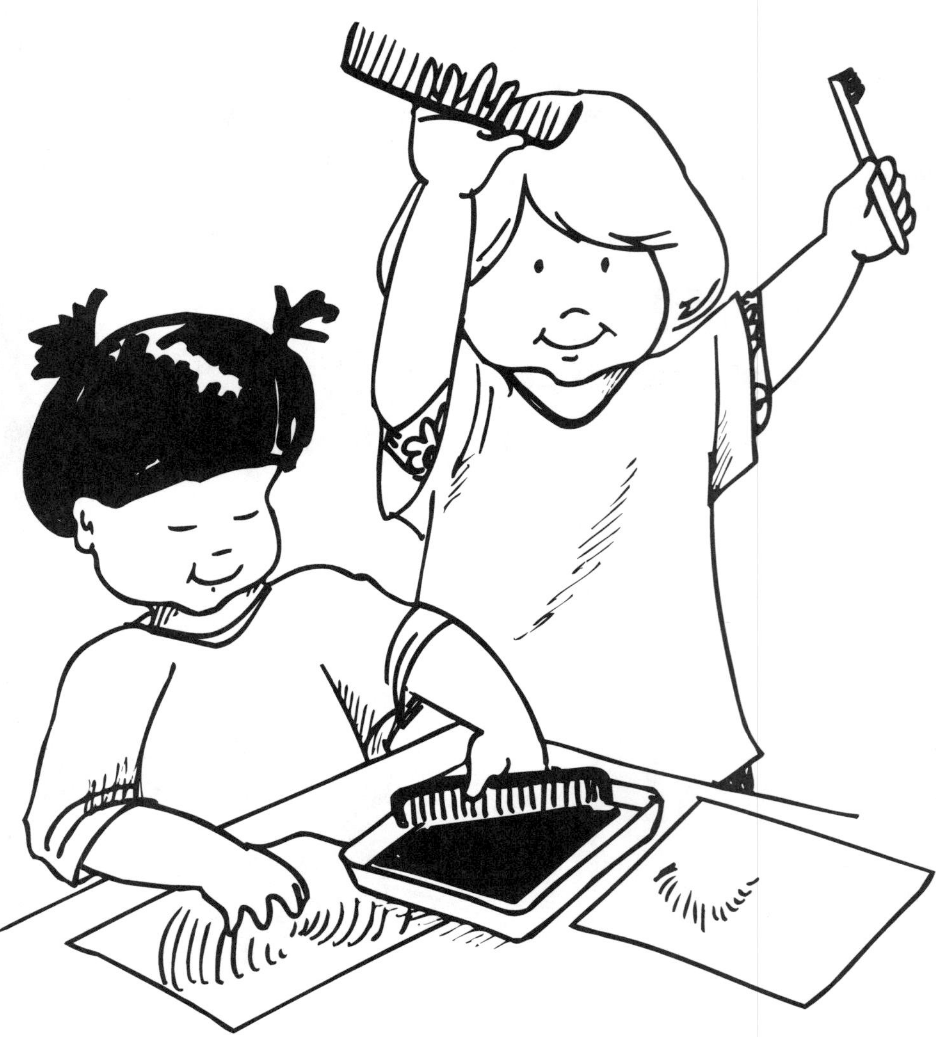

Oh, What a Feeling!

Collect Styrofoam trays from parents or go to the local grocery store and ask for them. Talk to the children about how relief prints are made and show them some relief prints or books with relief prints. (You can find these books at a local library.)

Set out paint on small foam trays. Then give each child a flat piece of Styrofoam. Provide the children with a variety of tools they can use to etch on their foam pieces such as toothpicks, craft sticks, paper clips, or pencils. Next, encourage the children to draw/etch a picture or design into their foam pieces by pressing down. After they have created their designs, let them take a small paint roller and dip it into their choice of paint. Have them roll the paint across their foam designs to create relief prints. Next, they can stamp their relief prints onto pieces of paper. Let them make as many prints on their papers as they choose.

Quick Tip
Invite a local artist to come talk to the children about relief prints.

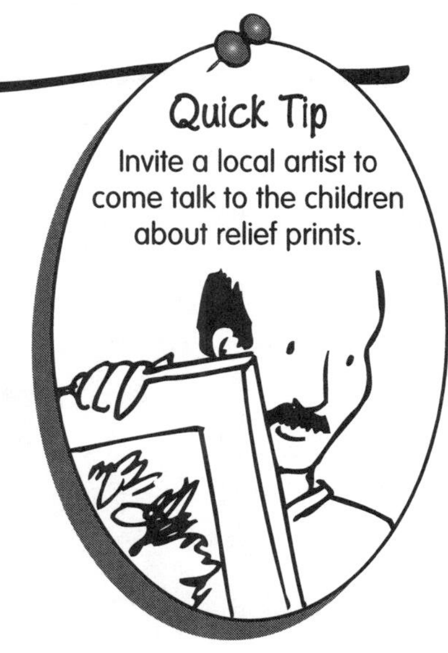

Another Idea
Let the children make greeting cards with their relief prints. Cut out interesting pieces of paper, cardboard, etc., for the children to use.

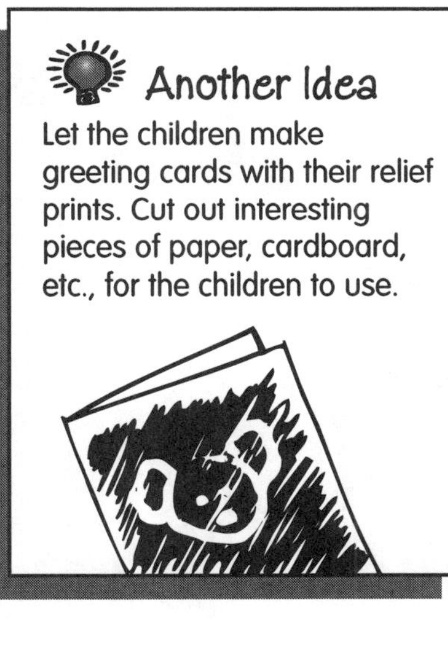

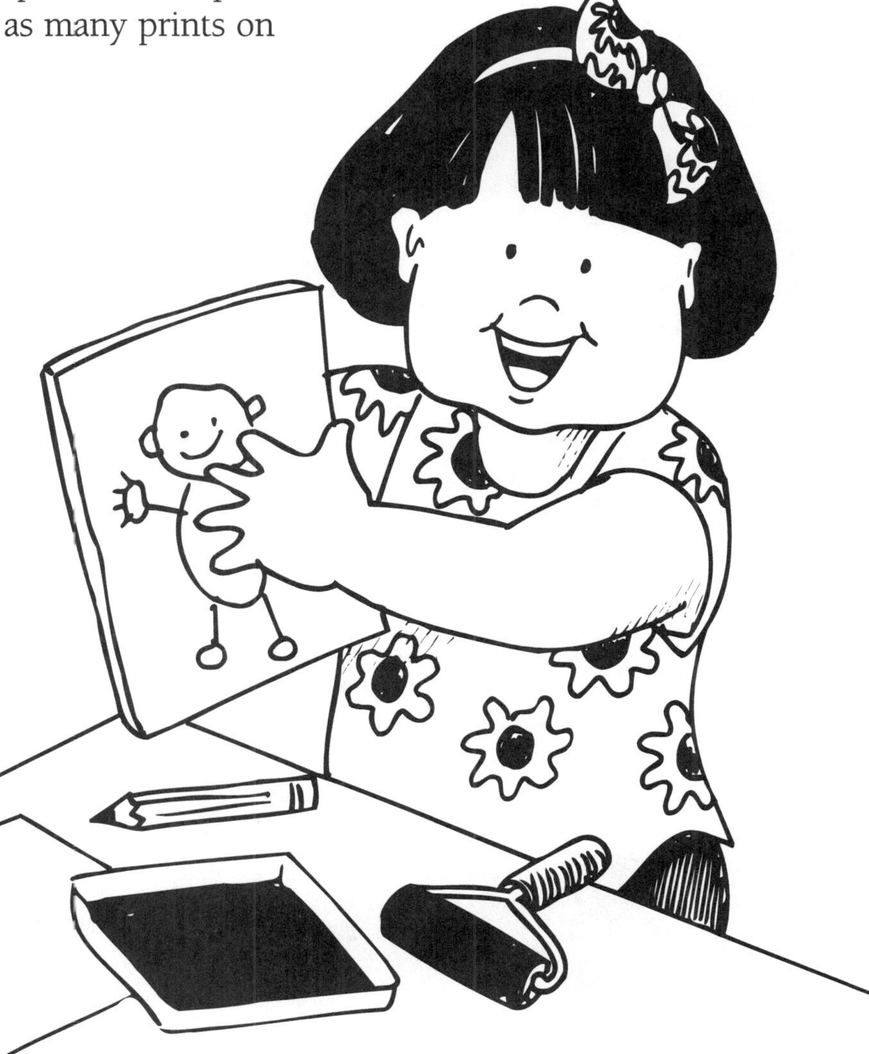

Footstep Fun

When you have collected a variety of shoes, set them in the art center. Next, set out large sheets of paper such as easel paper or newsprint. Put small amounts of paint on plastic trays. Have each child put on a smock and find a sheet of paper. Encourage the children to take a shoe and dip the bottom of the shoe in paint. Then they take the shoe and put the sole on the paper, push down, and lift to make a print. The children can then repeat the process using different shoes or the same shoes. Let them use different colors and have fun creating footsteps. After they are dry, display them in the room.

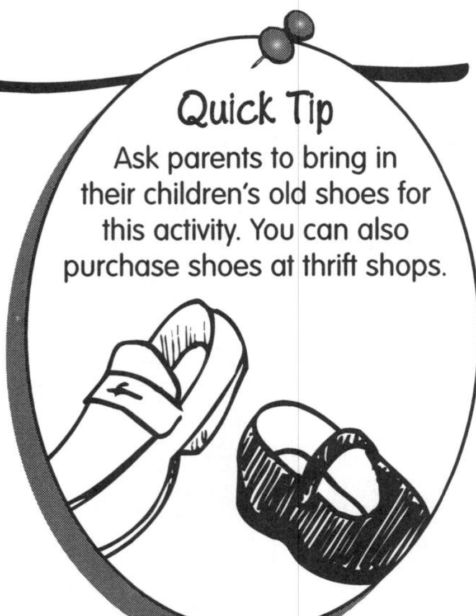

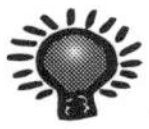

Another Idea

Purchase small latex gloves. Set out the gloves and some paint on trays and let the children dip their glove-covered hands in the paint. They can create handprints on paper.

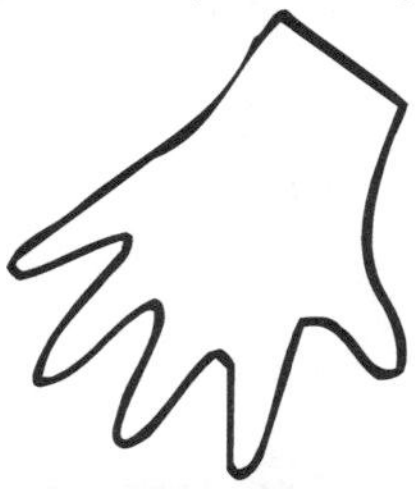

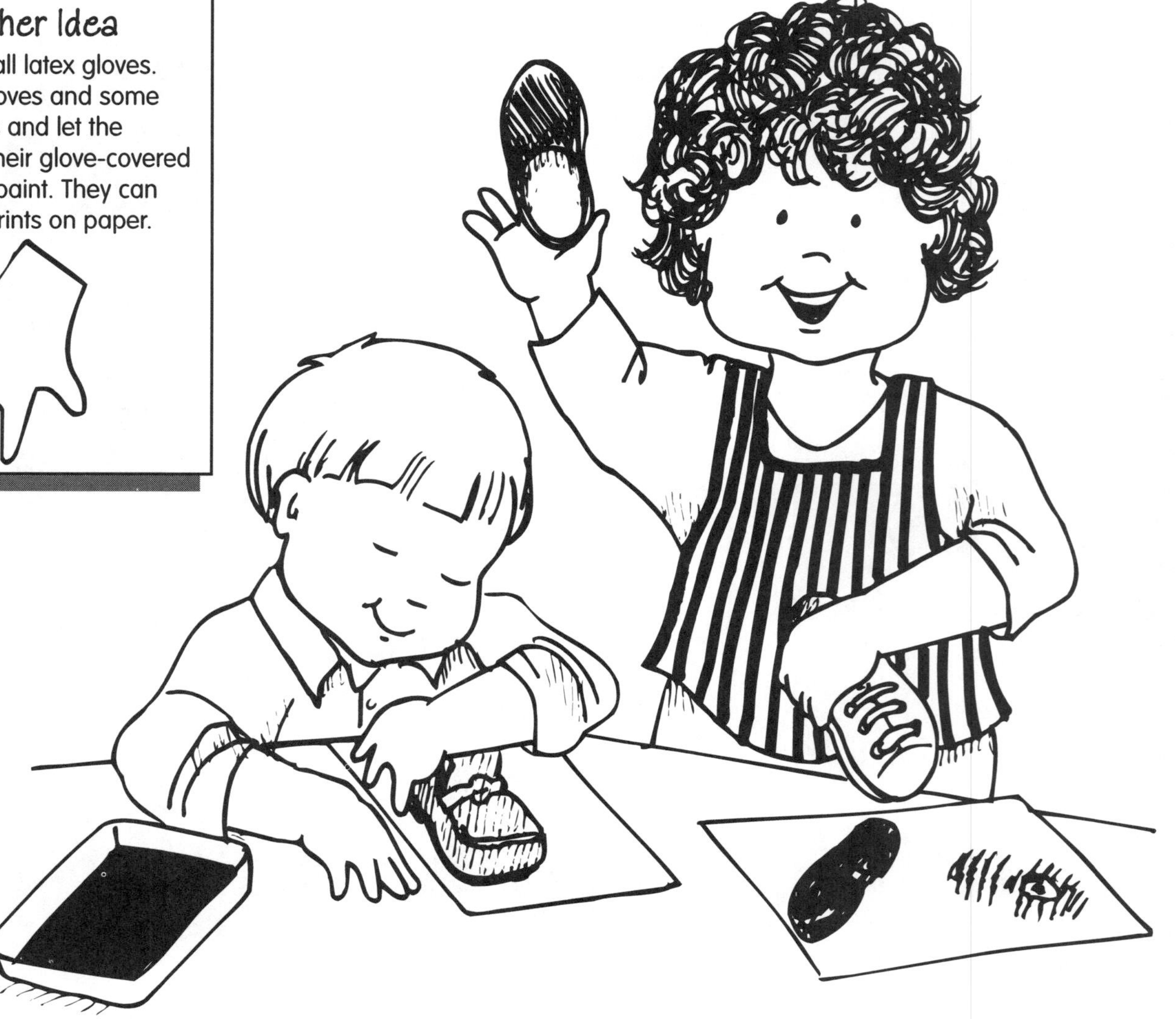

News Art

On a large table, set out a variety of paper the children can use for printing, such as newspaper, white tissue paper, white wrapping paper, etc. Set out stencils, rubber stamps, sponges, and any other materials along with paints and stamp pads. As the children are making their prints, they might enjoy pretending that they are printers working in a newspaper shop. Encourage the children to work in the print shop. You can set the print shop up for a week in the classroom and add to it throughout the week. Or, you may choose to set it up outside in an area that has a large table. Let the children's work dry and then have them write about their print projects. Create a bulletin board entitled "News Art."

Quick Tip

Invite someone from the local newspaper to come talk to the children and explain how a printing press works. You can usually get newsprint from newspaper companies.

Another Idea

Purchase a few sets of alphabet and number stamps along with some stamp pads from local discount stores. Set these items out along with paper, and let the children create cards, letters, and number art designs.

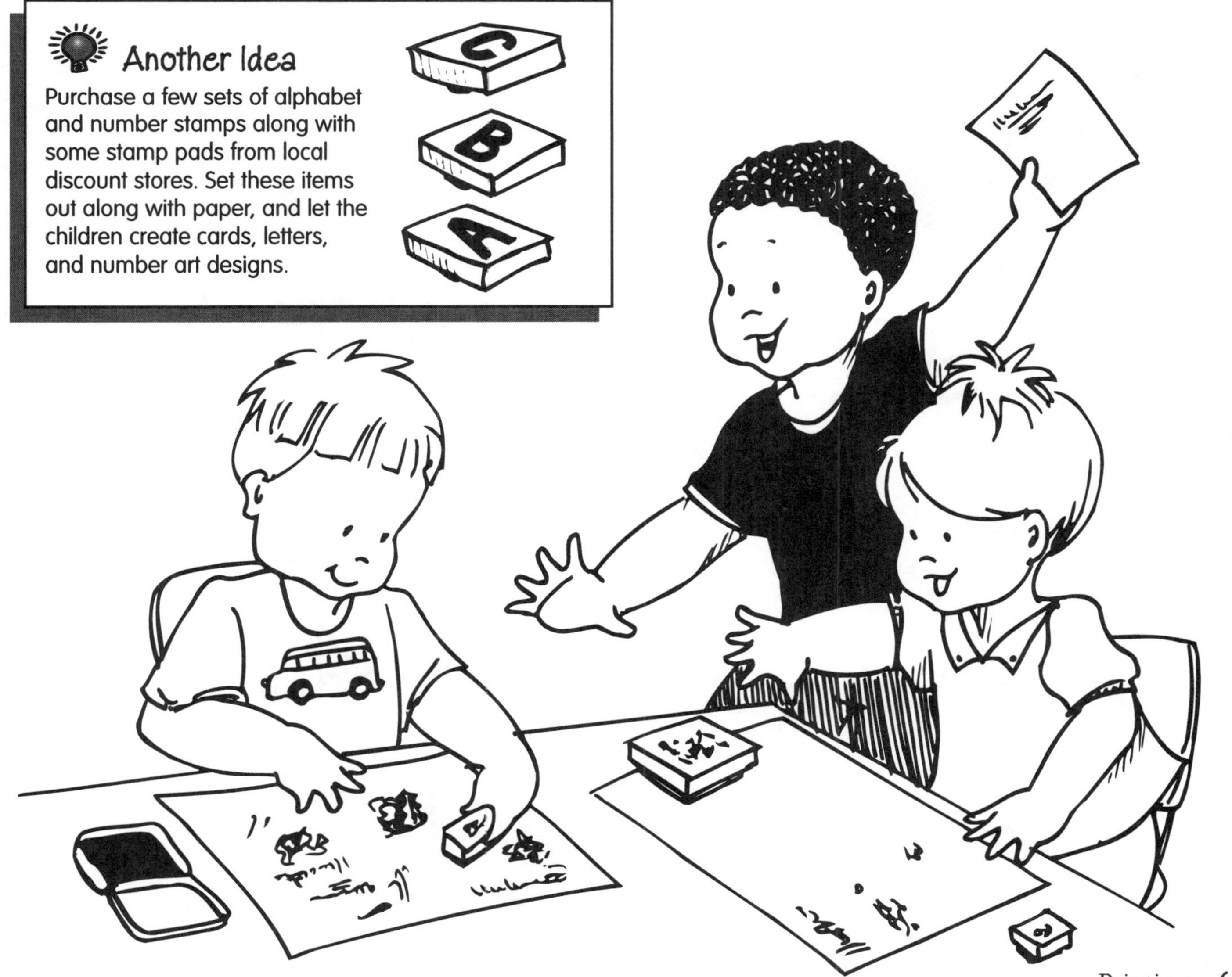

Celebration of Candles

Set out paper and paint in various colors on foam trays. Be sure to only put a small amount of paint on the trays to control the amount of paint the children will get on their hands. Also have some damp and dry paper towels the children can wipe their hands with after the project. Let the children roll a variety of candles in the paint and then gently roll them onto the paper. Let the prints dry. Then have the children go over their dried prints with other candle prints to see what happens.

Quick Tip

Candles come in a variety of shapes and sizes. Look for unique textured candles that can be rolled onto paper. Birthday candles, beeswax candles, tapered candles, tea candles, and many more candles work great for this unique art experience.

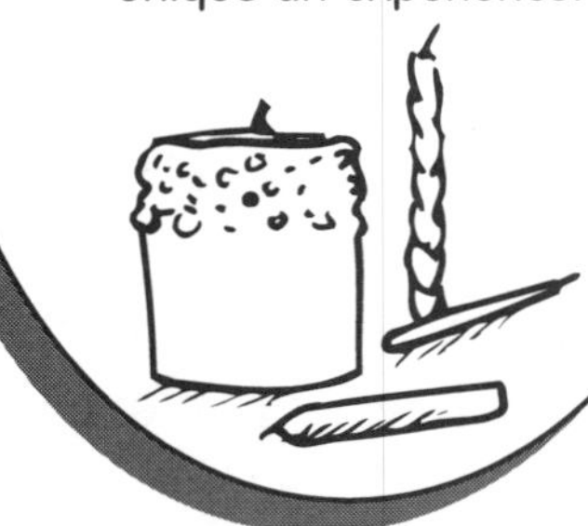

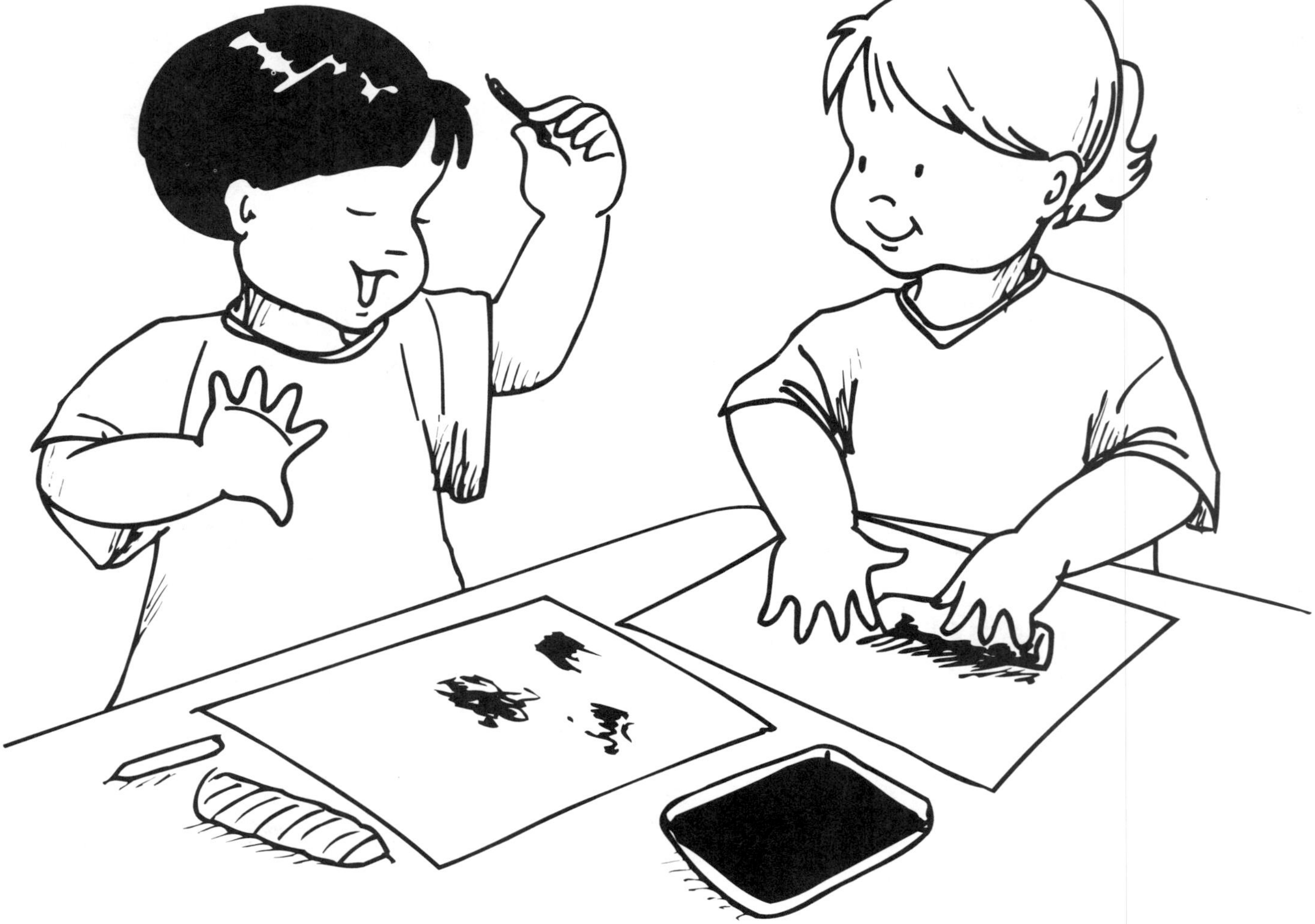

Rock and Roll Fun

Set out a variety of different colors of paint on foam trays, and set rocks and stones out next to the paint. Provide a variety of different kinds of materials the children can use, such as cardboard, paper, fabric, and tissue paper. Have the children select different shapes and sizes of rocks to dip in the paint and then make prints on their surfaces. Let the prints dry. Then encourage the children to draw with crayons or markers around the prints to give their art creations a different look.

Quick Tip

Call local plant nurseries and gravel companies to get free rocks and stones.

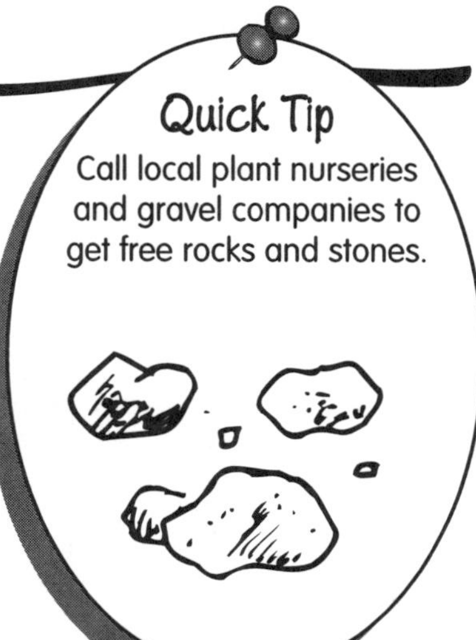

Another Idea

Gather seashells, bark, pine cones, acorns, leaves, and other nature objects the children can use to create prints. Set out the materials, and let the children create nature prints by dipping the objects into paint and then pressing them onto paper. Let the children select from a variety of different colors, textures, and shapes of paper.

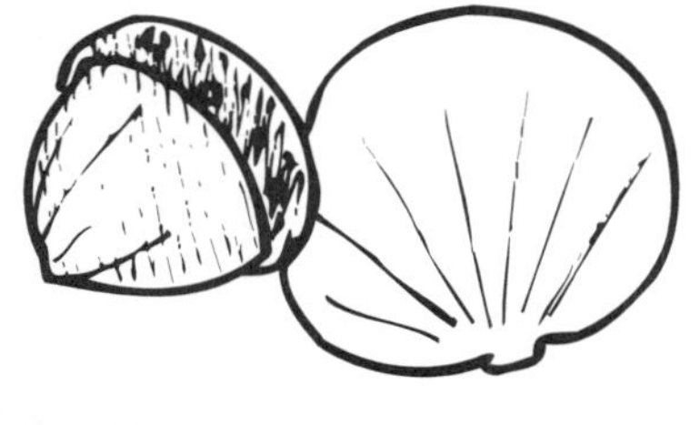

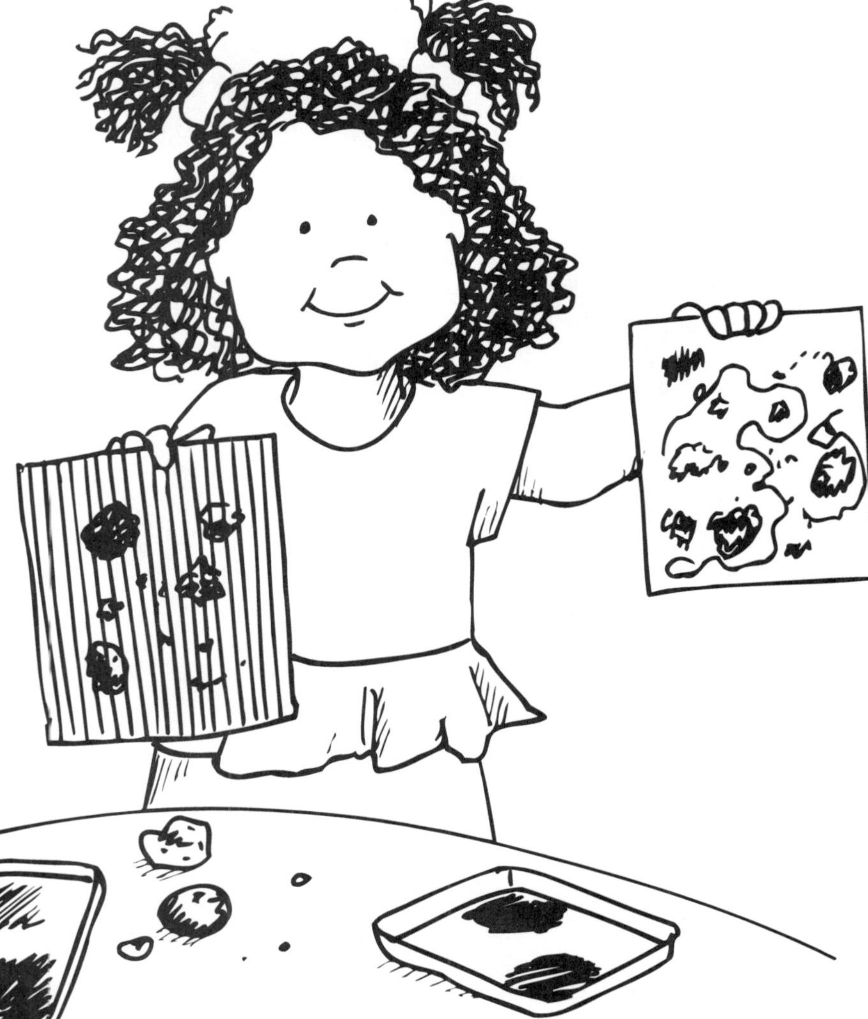

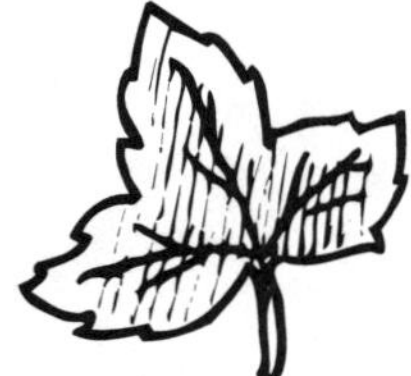

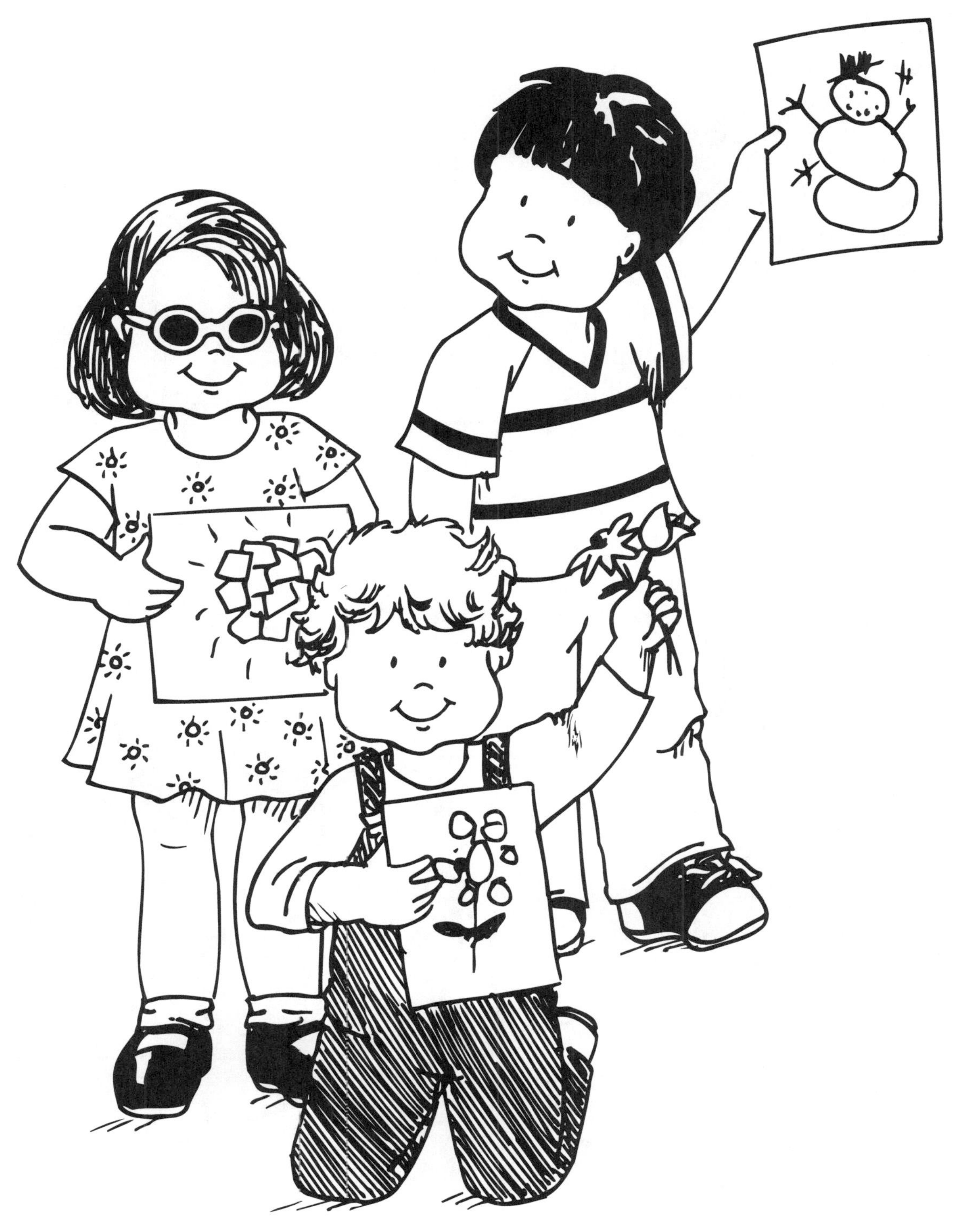

Seasonal

Seasonal Magic

Set out one empty, clear plastic liter water or soda bottle with a lid for each child. Let the children choose a small handful of items from 10 various items you provide in a collage box, such as glitter, sequins, buttons, beads, pebbles, shells, etc. (Provide seasonal items in the box as well.) As they choose the items, let them drop them into their bottles.

Next, help each child pour ¼ cup corn syrup into his or her bottle. Then the children can fill the rest of their bottles with water. Fasten the lids securely with duct tape. Let the children shake their bottles and watch their cool creations.

Quick Tip

Collect water bottles and clear plastic soda bottles from parents.

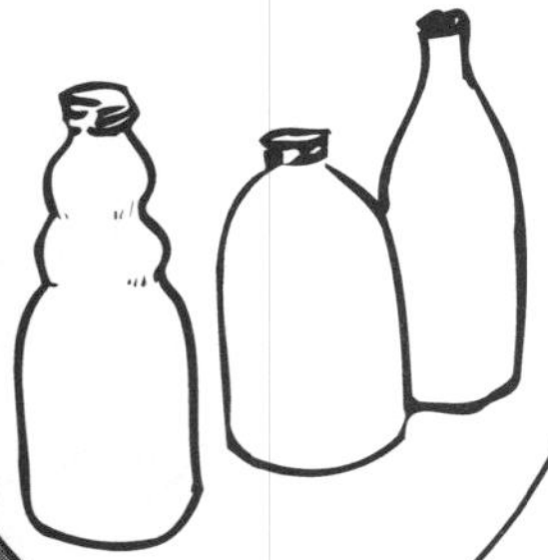

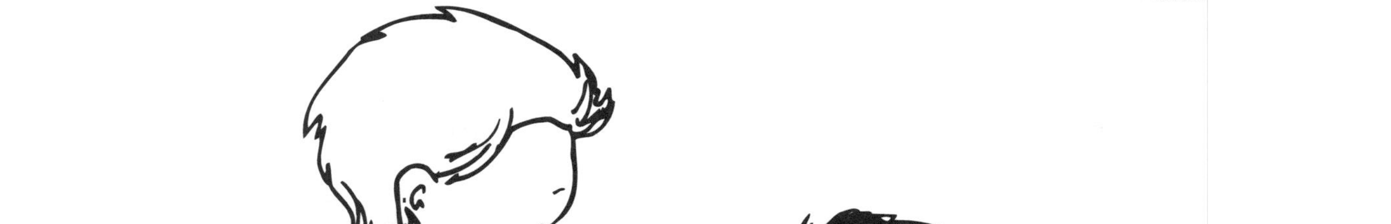

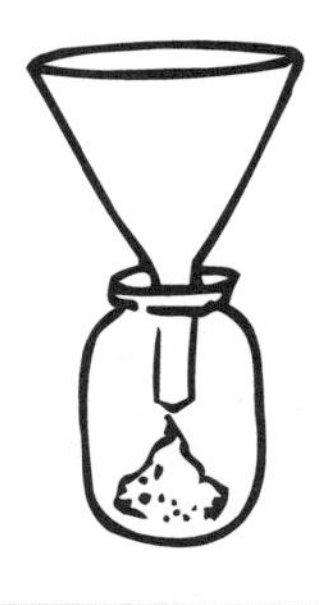

Another Idea

Prepare colored sand for the children to use by mixing 2 cups of sand with 3 tablespoons of food coloring. Place the sand in small tubs. Provide the children with funnels, spoons, and clear plastic bottles with lids. Encourage the children to scoop different colors of sand into their bottles using spoons and funnels.

Summer Suns

Gather red, orange, and yellow tissue paper, and cut it into 1" x 1" squares. Next, gather some tinsel if you have any available and one large sheet of paper for each child. Set out crayons, the tissue paper squares, paintbrushes, the large sheets of paper, and a glue/water mixture for each child. (glue/water mixture—5 tablespoons glue, 1 tablespoon warm water; Mix well.) Place the glue mixture in small cups.

Let the children draw a large circle (sun) on their papers. Then they can use the paintbrushes to spread glue on their suns. Next, the children can put different colors of tissue paper onto their suns and spread more glue on top of the tissue paper squares. Encourage the children to add more tissue paper of different colors if necessary. When they have completed their suns, they can then glue on tinsel or use crayons to make sun rays. Hang the colorful suns outside or inside for all to enjoy.

Quick Tip

Take the children outside to observe the sunshine if possible, or read stories about the sun to the children.

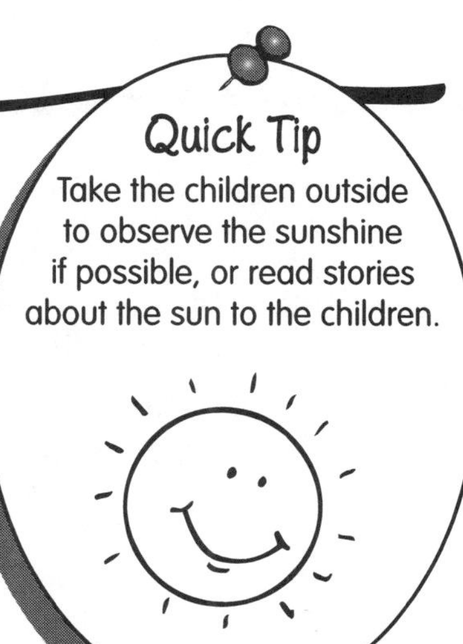

Another Idea

Using the same process, have the children make a tissue paper flower garden using assorted colors of tissue paper that you have cut into small sizes. Give them paper and let them draw big sunflowers, tulips, etc., on their papers. Then they can glue tissue paper on their drawings. Send these home for their parents to enjoy.

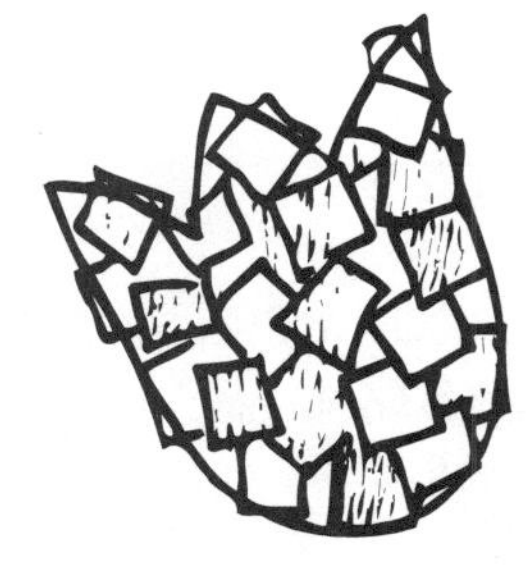

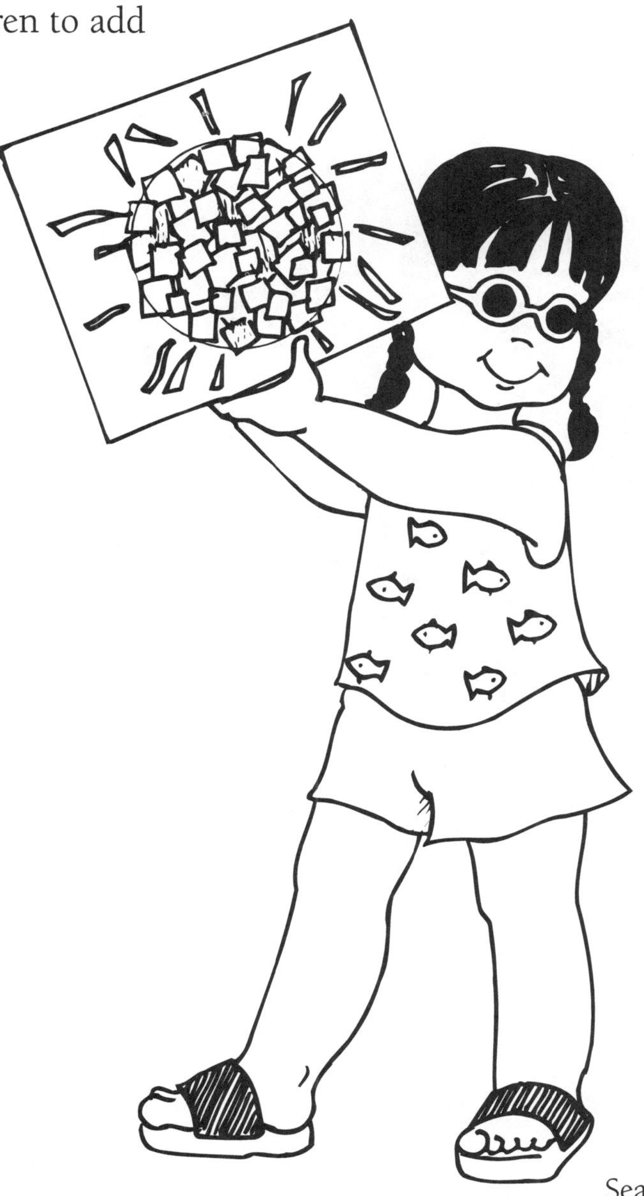

Fall Dried Flowers

Collect flowers, leaves, and other free gifts from nature. Let them dry in the classroom. Let the children choose and decorate a container using paper, tape, glue, etc. Then lay out all of the flowers and nature items. Let the children create arrangements you can display on tables and throughout the room.

Quick Tip

Ask someone from a local garden club to come in and talk with the children about flowers. Encourage families to bring in dried flowers for this project and to save plastic milk cartons, juice cans, and plastic cups.

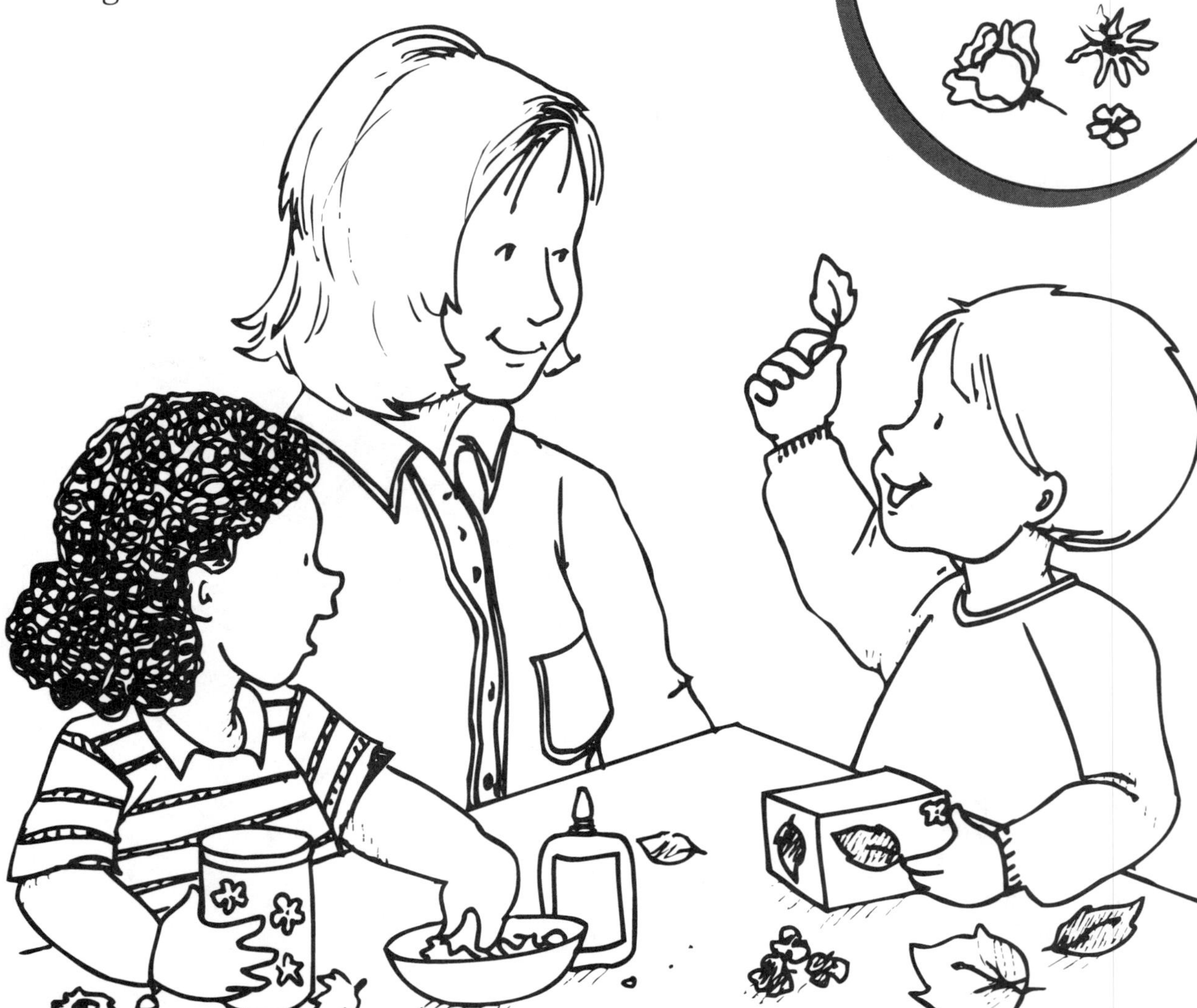

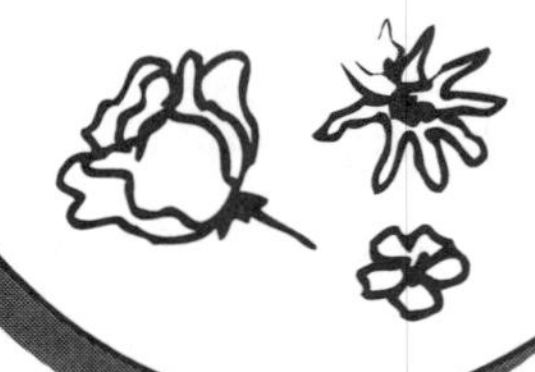

Another Idea

Let the children put colorful fall leaves onto clear self-stick paper and then attach them to the windows in the classroom. The children will enjoy looking at the leaves.

Winter Ice Painting

Ahead of time, prepare a variety of colored ice for all the children to use. To prepare, mix a small amount of paint with water, and pour the mixture into snow cone cups. (Use different colors of paint so the children can choose from a variety of colors.) Place each cone into an empty water bottle from which you have cut off the top. The cups will fit into the bottles and stand upright in the freezer. Let freeze overnight.

Set out large sheets of white butcher block paper (outside or inside) on a plastic shower curtain. Take the cones out of the freezer and tear off the paper. Let the children have a sensory experience by painting with the colored ice. Observe how they use the ice. They can draw with either end, make prints, and explore with others ways to express themselves using the colored ice. You might provide winter gloves for the children to wear if they choose to.

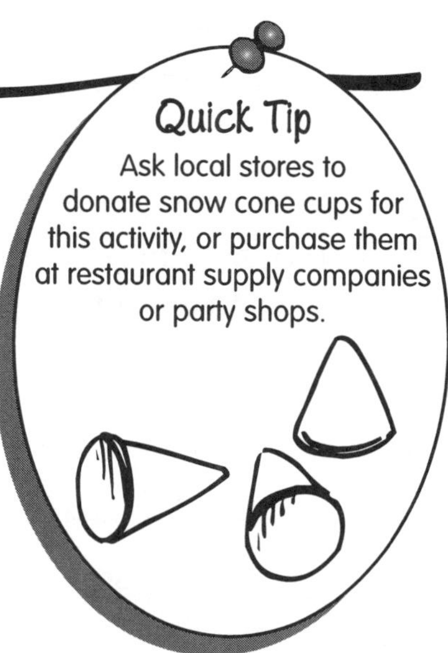

Quick Tip

Ask local stores to donate snow cone cups for this activity, or purchase them at restaurant supply companies or party shops.

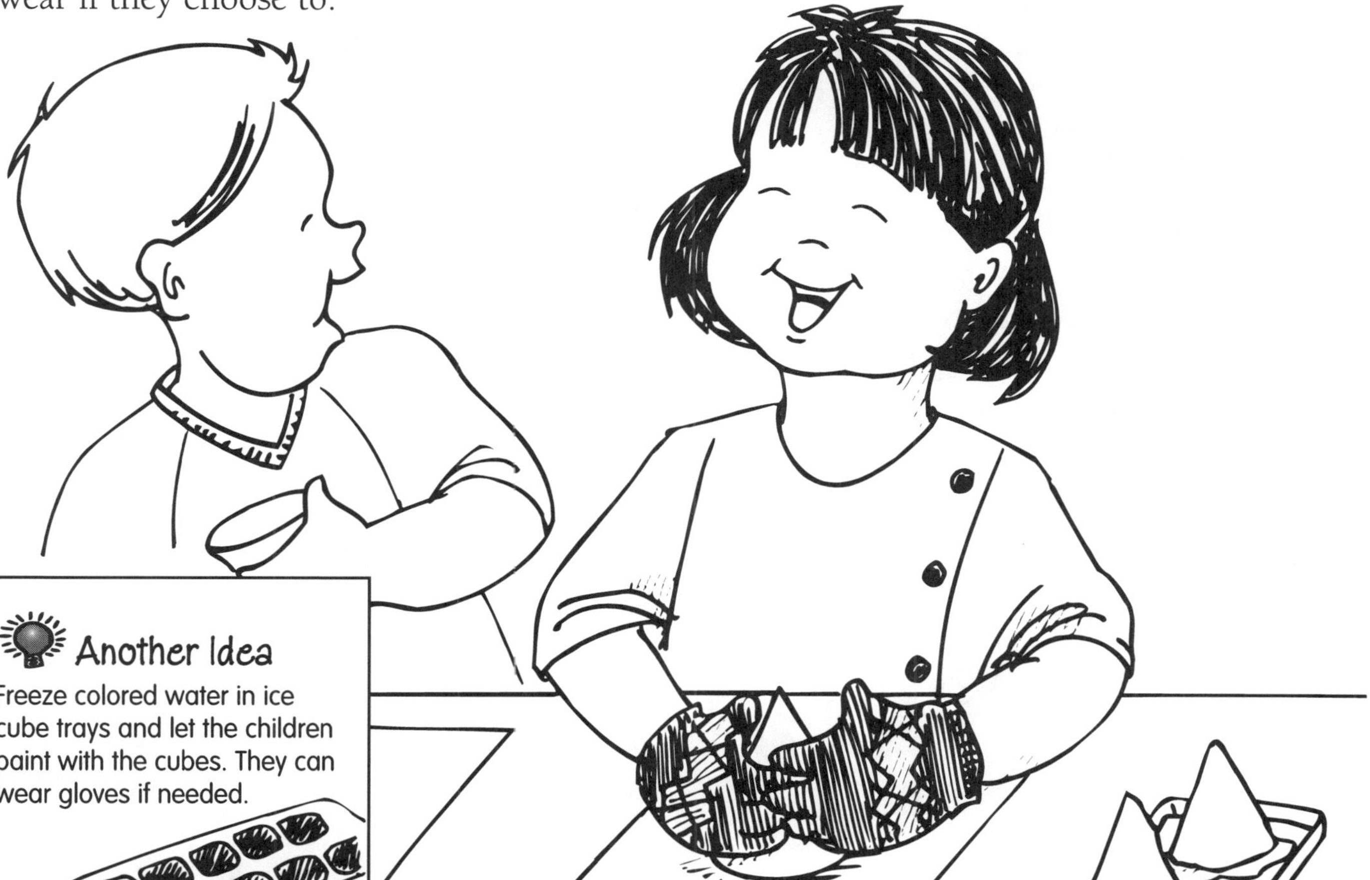

Another Idea

Freeze colored water in ice cube trays and let the children paint with the cubes. They can wear gloves if needed.

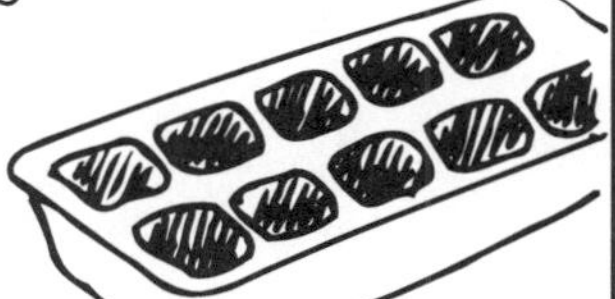

Frosted Art Fun

Mix 1 cup Epsom salts with 1 cup boiling water. Let cool. Have the children use crayons to draw on different shapes, colors, and textures of paper. When the Epsom salt mixture has cooled, give the children paintbrushes and let them paint over the pictures with the mixture. Crystals will appear on their papers. Hang them around other winter scenes that the children have created.

Quick Tip

Ask a pharmacist if he or she has any Epsom salts that the store might be discarding because of opened or damaged boxes that could be donated to your school.

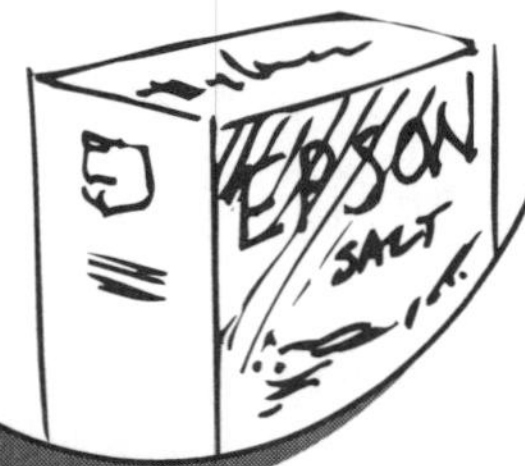

Another Idea

During the holidays, children love to make cards to give to friends and family members. Give the children construction paper, tinsel, and the Epsom salt mixture along with paintbrushes that they can use to make beautiful cards.

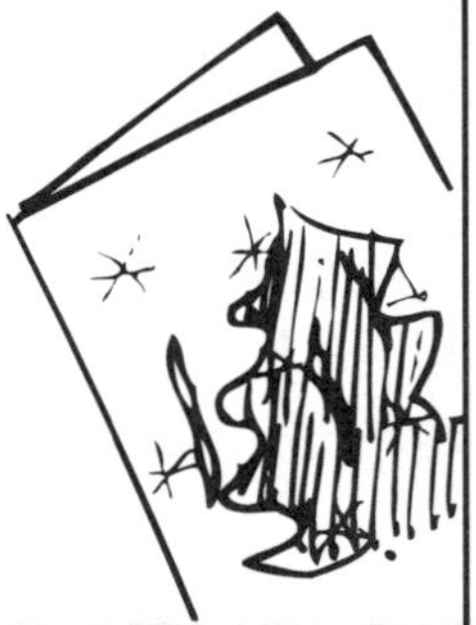

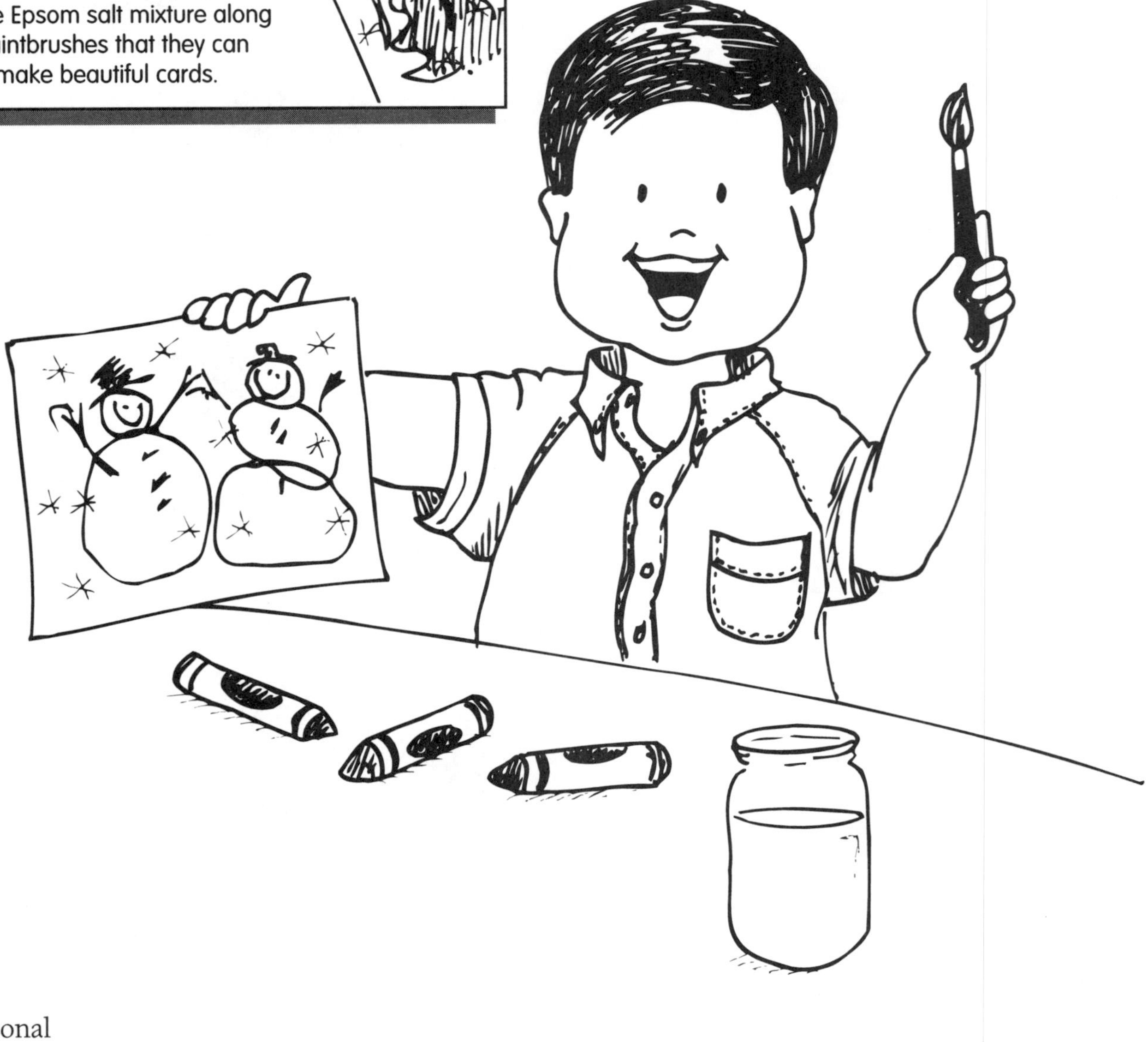

Spring Flower Power

Set out a variety of live flowers in the art center. Encourage the children to tell you about the flowers—how they smell, feel, their color, shape, etc. Next, set out large and small sheets of paper. Set out many different sizes of paintbrushes and paint in colors that are similar to the colors of the flowers you set out. Have the children paint colorful pictures of spring flowers.

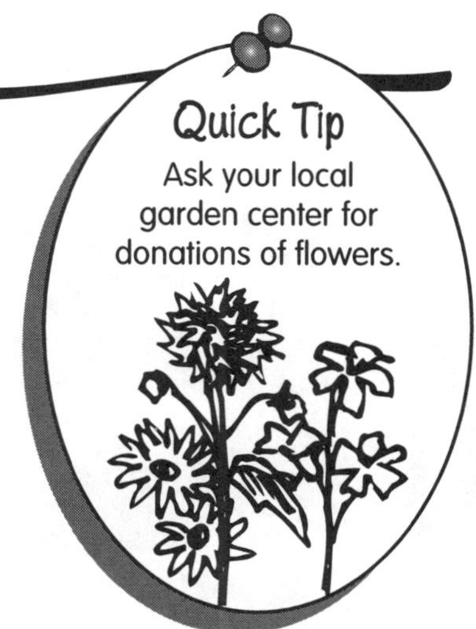

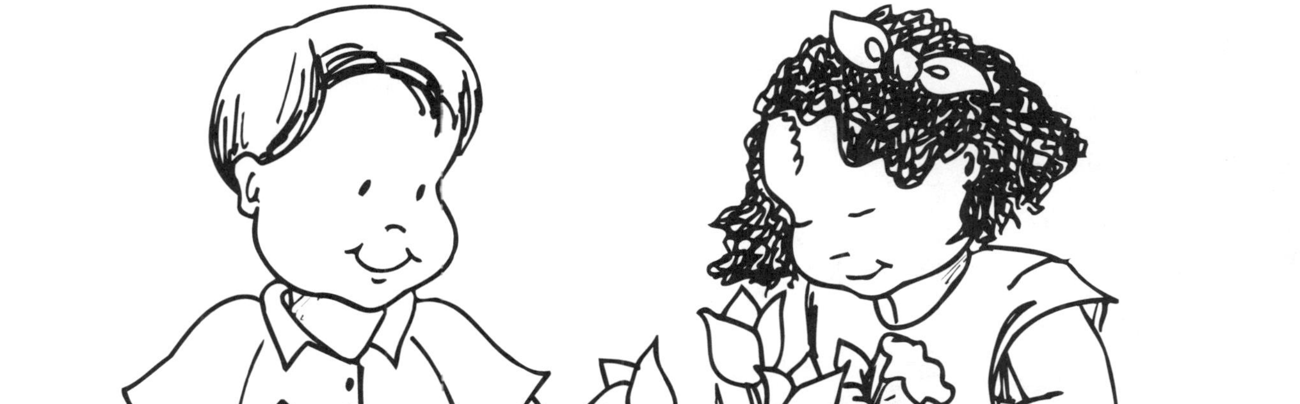

Another Idea

Cut many different flowers. Let the children create colorful flower arrangements to take home. They can place the flower arrangements in small plastic cups and place them on tables at home. What wonderful conversation pieces that can encourage family involvement!

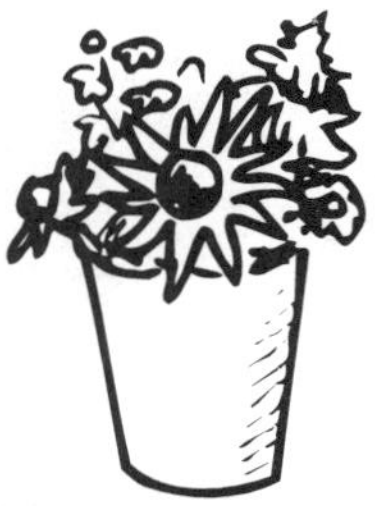